How To Raise
A Venture Capital Fund

The Essential Guide on Fundraising
and Understanding Limited Partners

Winter Mead

First Edition

Winter Mead, San Francisco, CA

How To Raise A Venture Capital Fund / Winter Mead. —1st ed.
Trade Paperback: 978-1-7362343-0-3
Hardcover: 978-1-7362343-1-0
eBook: 978-1-7362343-2-7

To my family, in particular Danesha and Jude,
who've supported this effort from the beginning

Contents

Foreword

Despite all of the writing on venture capital, there is a missing part of the literature. There has been no book written about raising a venture capital fund. It remains a secret to a few privileged venture capitalists who have gone through this fundraising process. Until now . . .

This book serves as a guidebook to raising a venture capital fund. It dives into the process of raising a venture capital fund, the how-tos, the unique language of the limited partner (LP) world, secrets of how LPs think about fund diligence and alignment, the best practices in fundraising, what works, and how you can best prepare for success.

I've written this book after spending a decade investing into venture capital funds at a $30B wealth management firm and a $160B technology company. I've been on both sides of the table, the VC and the LP side. I've been behind the scenes managing every aspect of the fundraising process, investing into 80 funds, and reviewing thousands of fund investments. I also co-founded a company that specifically focuses on co-building venture capital businesses, which includes helping VCs understand the intricate dynamics of raising a venture capital fund. After reading my book, you will gain the knowledge and insights gained from these experiences.

Why I Am Writing This Book

In the current economic wave, innovation and technology have begun to affect all industries and geographies in significant ways. Innovation is a global phenomenon, and venture capital has become known as a form of financing that enables innovation. People associate venture capital with the future of innovation and technology, and in some cases, with how society will ultimately function.

Companies funded by venture capital have become the most valuable companies in the world. In fact, Apple and Amazon both started as VC-backed businesses and became the first publicly listed companies to reach one trillion in valuation (a thousand billions!). These two businesses began because venture capitalists invested in visionary founders who were talented at business building.

Recently, the market has become increasingly large, fragmented, and obscure. My goal is to clarify the process of raising a venture capital fund. Knowing how to raise a venture capital fund is an essential step in enabling more innovation. My goal is to encourage and motivate future generations of venture capitalists to raise venture capital funds. My hope is that more venture capitalists will enable accelerated innovation, resulting in large, positive impacts on a global scale.

The nomenclature of a venture capitalist raising a fund, especially for first timers, can get complex, involving terminology, abbreviations, and acronyms. Here are just a few to get your head spinning: accredited investor, qualified purchaser, DPI, TVPI, IRR, LP, GP, Key Person clause, clawback, SWF, PPM, DDQ, ODD, LPA, and the list goes on. Confused yet?

I want to empower first time investors as well as people who want to learn more about the world of venture capital and the source of venture capital money. Readers should walk away with an understanding of what goes on behind the scenes with venture capitalists (referred to as VCs) and Limited Partners (referred to as LPs) during the fundraising process. The book will provide insights and perspectives from my experience as an institutional limited partner. If you have ambition and the willingness to commit to raising and managing a venture capital fund, then this is the book to help you succeed.

I will guide you through the process and help prepare you for raising your own venture capital fund—from making the initial decision to raising a fund to closing the fund. You will learn what it means to be a **venture capitalist** or a **limited partner** and the professional responsibilities attached to those titles. Are you ready for success? Then let's get started.

Venture Capital And The Main Players Involved In Raising A Venture Capital Fund

All the world's a stage, And all the men and women merely players; They have their exits and their entrances.

—William Shakespeare

What Is Venture Capital?

As David Swensen defines in his seminal book *Pioneering Portfolio Management*, venture capital is "providing financing and company building skills to start-up operations with the goal of developing companies into substantial, profitable enterprises."

Who are the main players in venture capital?

More importantly, venture capital is an ecosystem with three main players:

1. Entrepreneurs: who start and manage companies day-to-day.

2. Venture capitalists (VCs): who finance entrepreneurs.

3. Limited partners (LPs): who finance venture capitalists.

In this book, we will focus on the VCs and LPs and the relationship between the LP and the VC when the VC is raising a venture capital fund.

Who Are The Main Players In This Book?

Venture capitalists

Venture capitalists (VCs) manage a venture capital fund and make important decisions about when to make an investment and when to exit an investment. Their role may also include working closely with the companies in which they invest, such as providing strategic advice and helping with recruiting and hiring.

Are you an emerging or established VC?

LPs will distinguish between VCs who are relatively newer to investing (emerging VC) and those who have been actively investing for a longer period of time (established VC).

Emerging VC: An emerging VC typically refers to a VC that does not have a "proven" track record over a long period of time. A track record is a history of investments into companies. Usually the term "emerging VC" refers to any VC before her/his fourth fund, because it usually takes at least two or three funds for LPs to understand how good of an investor a VC is. At a high level, the common refrain of fund one is raised on relationships, fund two is raised on momentum and to support the manager when there is still little data, and fund three is raised on the data of fund one, which begins to determine for the LP whether the VC is good at investing.

Established VC: An established VC, on the other hand, has a proven track record because they have been investing into companies for a longer period of time and can point to their attribution and "success stories" of investing early into successful companies. Established VCs typically already have a brand in the venture capital market that is recognized by entrepreneurs and LPs, and they may also have sold one or several companies so there is a history of success. This book is not going to cover established VCs because they can raise capital more easily because of the established track records and relationships they already hold with LPs.

Does your background matter?

Backgrounds matter but can vary. Three famous examples of VCs with different backgrounds are Mike Moritz (a VC at Sequoia), Bill Gurley (Benchmark), and Marc Andreessen (A16Z). Mike Moritz has a background in journalism, Bill Gurley has a background as a Wall Street research analyst, and Marc Andreessen has a background as a software engineer and entrepreneur. In terms of the right background or set of experiences for a VC, there is no right or wrong recipe. Rather, VCs can come from many different backgrounds and be successful, meaning they generate return on capital for their LPs. It comes down to being able to show LPs you have mastered the craft of venture capitalism and can source, access, manage, and eventually make money persistently by investing as a venture capitalist.

Limited partners

Limited Partners (LPs) are the people and institutions that invest into venture capitalists. A close friend of mine and a long-term VC defined it well in a joking manner: "limited partners are not called 'limited' because of their intellectual capacity and skillsets; rather, the term 'limited' refers to the fact that LPs have limited liability when investing into a VC fund." That is, LPs are limited in how involved they can be in the day-to-day operations of a venture capital firm. Being too involved in the day-to-day operations of a VC firm can change the legal liability status of a limited partner, so it is best for the LP to defer to the VCs who manage the day-to-day operations of the VC firm. The following list includes the most popular types of LPs. We will not dive too deep into any particular type of LP, but it is wise to note that LPs have different preferences and reasons for investing into VC funds.

Banks

Banks can have dedicated teams that invest in venture capital funds, usually through an investment division at the bank or through affiliated wealth managers. Banks can invest for strategic reasons (e.g., financial technology) or financial returns. An example of a bank that invests in venture capital funds is Goldman Sachs.

Corporation (or corporate investor)

A corporate investor can include an organization from a wide variety of industries, including software. An example of a corporate that invests in venture capital funds is Google.

Endowment

An endowment is a non-profit organization that supports an organization, such as a school. Examples of well-known endowments that are LPs in venture capital include Yale University, Princeton University, and Stanford University, among others. Endowments can also be other organizations, such as churches. Endowments share lots of similarities with foundations as non-taxable, donor-backed organizations that support charitable efforts, though there are some operational, legal, and tax differences between the two that we will not go into in this book. Unlike foundations, endowments can sometimes have multiple constituencies and therefore be more political. Endowments can also have fewer restrictions than foundations and therefore at the margin make riskier investments, which can be a positive for those looking to raise risk capital for a venture capital fund.

Family Office (FO)

Family offices are private wealth management advisors that serve a single family or ultra-high net worth individual, which, by definition, is an individual with at least $30 million to invest. Yes, some families have so much money that there are companies formed to serve that one family in terms of managing and diversifying their wealth.

Fund-of-funds

A fund-of-funds is an investment strategy that involves investing in other investment funds: a fund to invest in funds. For their own LPs, fund-of-funds offer broader diversification in venture capital.

Foundation

A foundation is a non-governmental, non-profit organization that is tax-exempt. Foundations share lots of similarities with endowments as non-taxable, donor-backed organizations that support charitable efforts, though there are some operational, legal, and tax differences between the two that we will not go into in this book.

High Net Worth Individual

Sometimes high net worth individuals are referred to as high net worths, HNWs, or HNWIs. Sometimes high net worth individuals are broken up into tiers, including UHNWs, which stands for ultra-high net worths. The important part is to think about how much investable money an individual has to commit to your fund over time. There are even legal definitions to make sure individuals don't spend all of their money on illiquid venture capital. For example, a HNW has to be an accredited investor, defined in Rule 501 of Regulation D (see SEC website for the technical definition). That is, to invest in venture capital funds, there are legal rules to ensure the HNWI can cover these invest-ments without causing severe adverse effects for the HNWI if her investments lose all their value.

Insurance Companies

Insurance companies collect premiums that are invested before pay-outs, including investments into venture capital funds.

Multi-family Offices (MFO)

In addition to single family offices, there are also multi-family offices, which are private wealth management advisors that serve more than one ultra-high net worth family.

Outsourced Chief Investment Officer (OCIO)

Outsourced chief investment officers, also known as outsourced CIOs or OCIOs, are companies that manage and make investment decisions on behalf of client portfolios. These clients can be ultra-high net worth individuals, family offices, or other investment institutions, such as pension funds, endowments, or foundations. OCIOs can make invest-ment decisions on behalf of their clients, for example, deciding to invest in venture capital funds.

Pension Fund

Pension funds can include corporate pensions, public pensions, and other types of pensions. The value of pension funds in just the U.S. alone is massive, with the total of all U.S. pension funds valued in the trillions of dollars. For this reason, pension funds typically only invest in larger venture capital funds.

Sovereign Wealth Fund (SWF)

A sovereign wealth fund, also known sometimes as a sovereign investment fund, is a state-owned investment fund that can invest in alternative assets such as venture capital. Countries can have one SWF or multiple SWFs; for example, Norway has two main SWFs, and Singapore has two main SWFs. SWFs can be very large, too; for example, one of the SWFs controlled by Norway is valued at over $1 trillion. Because of their size, sometimes SWFs can invest billions of dollars into venture capital funds at a time. When interacting with smaller sized venture capital funds, SWFs typically require a specific mandate to invest in venture capital, or they need to have some strategic reason to invest in venture capital.

Venture Capital Funds

Wait, what? VCs invest into other VCs? Yes, this is actually fairly common, though the check sizes being invested by the venture capital funds can vary, though they are typically smaller than other types of LPs. VCs invest to strengthen relationships with other VCs in which they are investing, getting information flows such as which companies are doing well and organization best practices.

These are the main types of LPs you will encounter when raising a venture capital fund. However, this list is not exhaustive and does not account for all of the financial intermediaries that have relationships with these LPs and help invest the LPs' capital on their behalf.

When you finally set out on your journey to raise a venture capital fund, you will realize that there are many other types of investors, wealth managers, and financial types that can and will invest in venture capital funds.

When you approach these limited partners, note the differences in strategies and opinions. Some want 3x return on their investment; some want 5x. Some believe that investing in a seed stage focused fund is the right strategy to achieve outsized returns. Others may believe that investing in the "top 5" venture capital funds—that is, the funds with brand names and a long historical track record, also known as established funds—is the way to invest in venture capital, even if these funds are billions of dollars in assets under management (AUM). It is the VC's job to find out the investment interests of the LP by asking direct questions. This should be done as early as possible. If the LP cannot answer the questions clearly, then it may be time to focus on discussions with other LPs who can.

Why Do LPs Invest In VCs?

There are several reasons why limited partners invest in venture capital funds. First and foremost, limited partners are looking to invest capital into venture capital firms and make a return on their investment. Venture capital has traditionally been an attractive investment because of high returns for investors over a longer period of time.

Limited partners that invest in venture capital funds get exposure to venture capital without having to set up a team and dedicate human resources to sourcing and investing directly into companies, which can be more expensive and time intensive.

There are also other reasons for LPs to invest in venture capital funds. For example, some LPs may view investing into a venture capital fund as strategic to their corporate strategy and are looking to glean insights into a particular industry. Limited partners also may be looking to increase the number of direct investments they have in their portfolios; therefore, they view investing in venture capital funds as a "sensor network," where they can source companies to invest in at later investment rounds.

Still other LPs may be looking to start their own direct investment strategy. In order to learn about best practices in direct investing, they invest in venture capital funds as a limited partner. This can be positive for VCs in the short term because they will have engaged limited partners who have an interest in being an investor in the fund and a potential co-investor in portfolio companies. In the long term, when limited partners learn enough to start their own direct investment strategy, they may stop being a limited partner in future funds.

Limited partners known as Institutional Limited Partners (ILPs) invest into venture capital funds as a part of a larger investment strategy at an institution that may invest in other asset classes, such as hedge funds, public markets, or real estate. For the ILPs, the expectation is that the VC fund investment will offer diversification and outperform these other asset classes (over a long period of time) by investing in a fund that has invested in the next great fast-growing technology company, such as Apple, Amazon, or Google. If limited partners invest in a great-performing VC fund, the LPs can get a significant return that they otherwise would not have been able to get through other asset classes. The historical data shows that investing into venture capital (as part of a larger portfolio) will beat public market returns by about 5%, or 500 basis points over a 20-year period. Compounding that outperformance over 20 years, an LP can achieve significant returns all by accessing the right VC funds.

What Is The Legal Structure Of A Typical Venture Capital Fund?

For the legalese aficionados, get ready for some bronco-bucking entertainment! For all others, bear with me or skip ahead. Let's go one layer deeper to introduce the basic legal structure of a venture capital fund in the United States that raises money from limited partners.

To start, a VC sets up a legal entity called a **Management Company**, usually a Limited Liability Company (LLC), and a **General Partner**, also usually an LLC. The General Partner LLC has all the rights and responsibilities for managing a **Limited Partnership**, which is yet *another* legal entity managed by the VCs and consists of one or more limited partners as investors. LPs commit to the Limited Partnership.[1]

The Management Company, General Partner, and Limited Partnership are chosen for specific operational, tax, and logistical reasons.

The Management Company

- Limits the liability of the VC because it is an LLC

- Receives the management fees from funds that have been raised

- Pays for the operations of the fund, such as office lease, salaries, benefits, etc.

- Controls the formation of a successor fund

- Remains permanently as long as the VC is in business

The General Partner[2]

- Manages the Limited Partnership (see below)

- Technically is the entity responsible for making decisions of which companies to invest in

- Limits the liability of the VC because it is an LLC

- Allows for preferential tax status for the VC, including carried interest treated as capital gains

[1] This may get confusing because the two terms limited partner and limited partnership appear similar, so be aware of context! Also, LPs can technically invest to own part of the Management Company and/or the General Partners. Generally, though, LPs commit money to a VC by committing to the Limited Partnership.

[2] While advising where you should set up the General Partner is outside the scope of this book, it is recommended to speak with your lawyer about the optimal location to set up your venture capital fund to protect you, your investments, and optimize the tax treatment of your fund.

- Usually created for each new venture capital fund

The Limited Partnership

- Is a fancy term for the legal entity into which the LPs invest

- Is the main entity that makes investments into portfolio companies

- Must have at least one VC at the helm, and at least one limited partner

- Limits the liability of the limited partner

- Allows the limited partner to share in any profits made

- Is governed by the Limited Partnership Agreement, or LPA, which is the binding agreement between the VC and LP (the LPA will be discussed in more depth later)

What Are The Mechanics Of Investing Into A Venture Capital Fund?

Limited partners commit to a venture capital fund and become responsible for providing capital to the VC. This is a very important concept: the difference between a capital commitment and an investment when talking about how limited partners invest. For example, when a VC invests in a company, all of the money is wired into that company at once. However, when an LP invests, there is a two-part process of investing into the venture capital fund: the commitment and when the money is actually sent.

The first part of the process is the capital commitment, which refers to the total amount of capital the LP is liable for. If the LP makes a one million dollar commitment to a venture capital fund, the VC does not receive the money all at once.[3] Rather, the VC requests the limited partner to pay a certain percentage of the committed capital in increments over time. In industry jargon, the VC makes a "capital call" requesting or "calling" capital from the limited partner.[4] Therefore, a limited partner makes a capital commitment and then invests that capital over time, usually over the initial few years of a fund when the VC is making new investments and follow-on investments in her best companies. This period of time to make initial investments is referred to as the "investment period." The length of the fund is referred to as the "investment term." The VC typically cannot invest into new companies after the investment period; she can invest into the companies she has already invested in as follow-on investments.

After a VC makes a capital call, the LP is then legally required by the Limited Partnership Agreement (LPA), which is just the contract governing the VC fund, to send the VC capital. These capital calls will occur routinely throughout the duration of the fund on an ad hoc basis. Generally, the VC will call capital from the LP when making a new investment or to cover fees associated with the venture capital fund, such as management fees and operational fees, including accounting or auditing fees. The LP is legally contracted to pay these capital calls within an agreed upon amount of time, typically within ten business days of the capital call.

Most venture capital funds are structured as ten year legal entities.[5] The truth is that most venture capital funds will operate for longer than ten years. Typically, this is because some companies will take longer to grow, and the timing of the

---

[3] While the LPA may enable the VC to ask for all of the capital at once, he/she almost always will usually not do so because of how it impacts fund performance numbers, such as internal rate of return (IRR), which is important to raise additional venture capital funds in the future.

[4] The LP is legally contracted to pay these capital calls by the VC, typically within 10 business days of the capital call, or be subject to penalties, such as fines, or worse, getting removed as an investor in the fund.

[5] This is true for the United States; however, in other countries, the term life of the fund may differ. For example, in China, the term life of the fund can be shorter, such as seven years for venture capital funds.

exits of the portfolio companies cannot be forced right at the end of the fund life.

While the intention of the VC is to exit portfolio companies before the end of the fund, some companies may not sell before the end of the ten years. Usually, the contract between the VC and the LP allows for VCs under their own discretion to extend the fund life for two or three years if the VC needs more time to sell the companies in the VC portfolio. If the fund still needs to exist to hold portfolio companies after the extension, permission is usually required by the limited partner.

It should also be noted that although the fund life is ten years, the venture capitalist is only legally allowed to make investments over a shorter term, usually before the end of the fifth year. It is structured this way so that the companies have time to grow and mature.

According to industry data, the time from initial investment to exit is typically between five and eight years, so if a venture capitalist is making a new investment four years into the fund, the company may just be ready to sell or "exit" at the end of the fund life.

An "exit" refers to the VC getting money back for an investment in the following three ways:

- Selling the company in a merger or acquisition (M&A)

- Listing the company on the public market, usually via an initial public offering (IPO)[6]

- Secondary sale, which means selling the shares the VC owns of the company via a sale to another investor willing to pay for those shares in a private market transaction

---

[6] There are other means becoming more popular to list VC-backed companies on public stock exchanges, such as direct listings (DLs) and special purpose acquisition companies (SPACs), though going into these is outside the scope of this book.

After the venture capital fund's portfolio companies grow and exit, then the VCs have two choices—re-invest the capital into the VC fund or distribute the proceeds back to LPs. Re-investing the capital means the VC can use the exit proceeds; that is, the money from the sale is used to re-invest in other companies. However, if the exit occurs later in the fund life, then the VC most likely will distribute the proceeds or send the money back to the LPs.

VCs work for management fees and shared profits from the sale of the portfolio companies. Thus, VCs will keep a portion of the exit proceeds, usually between twenty to thirty percent of the profits. The VC will then send the remaining amount back to LPs, who in turn may re-invest the money back into venture capital. When working well, venture capital is a virtuous cycle of LPs investing in VCs, VCs sending money back to LPs, and LPs re-investing that capital back into VCs.

Prologue: The Four Phases Of Fundraising

While there is no one right way to raise a VC fund, there is definitely a general process to follow to make your life easier as a first timer tackling this new opportunity.

In the spirit of saving time and simplifying this complex and obscure part of the VC market, I'm providing a framework to think about fundraising, dividing the fundraising process into four phases:

Phase 1: Planning

Chapter 1: Self-Evaluation And Deciding On The Path Of A VC

Chapter 2: Design Your Fund's Investment Strategy

Chapter 3: Plan And Prepare Your Fundraising Materials

Chapter 4: Creating A Fundraising Plan — Targeting LPs, Pre-Marketing The VC Fund, And Maintaining A Flexible Mindset

Phase 2: Fundraising

Chapter 5: Reaching Out To And Interacting With Limited Partners

Chapter 6: Due Diligence

Chapter 7: Building Your Limited Partner Base

Phase 3: Closing The Fund

Chapter 8: Setting Business Terms, Negotiating The LPA, And The Side Letter

Chapter 9: Logistics Of Closing A Venture Capital Fund

Phase 4: LP Relations & Raising The Next Fund

Chapter 10: Managing The LP Relationship After Closing The Fund

Each one of these phases should be viewed as a distinct part of the fundraising process.

Phase 1 is primarily about planning. In this phase, you are self-evaluating, determining your initial team and investment strategy, and developing materials while seeking feedback from trusted friends, colleagues, advisors, and LPs who can help you iterate on your fund product.

Phase 2 is the actual work of fundraising, which is largely a sales process of finding, qualifying, and selling your fund product to prospective LPs who will invest in the fund. You will also be exposed to the LP perspective of conducting due diligence on your fund. There are a number of key considerations when fundraising that will be made clear during these chapters.

Phase 3 is about going deeper with the sub-set of LPs that have indicated interest in investing in your fund. You will have to negotiate business terms and create the legal documents to make your fund a reality.

Phase 4 is about investor management. Once someone invests, that is not the end of the relationship. Rather, it's the beginning. You need to now manage your investors with required engagements and communications and ideally scale your firm as you perform and strengthen those relationships.

PHASE 1: PLANNING

CHAPTER 1

Self-Evaluation And Deciding On The Path Of A VC

Without reflection, we go blindly on our way, creating more unintended conse-quences, and failing to achieve anything useful.

—Margaret Wheatley

Fundraising Mindset

Are you ready? How should you evaluate your readiness and positioning?

At some point, you have to make a conscious decision to raise a venture capital fund. This decision should be thought through carefully before embarking on the fundraising journey. For a first-time fund manager, this means starting a business that you plan to scale up over a long period of time. Raising a fund takes serious dedication. Your fund should match your experience and represent who you are, what you have done, and what you want to continue to do.

Recognize The Reality

Can you commit an extended period of time to a venture capital fund?

If so, then raising a venture capital fund may be for you! While it is not the only qualification, being able to take on a long-term commitment is an important factor in becoming a fiduciary of other people's money. Raising money, especially if you expect to raise it from institutional LPs, is not a side project. It is a full-time investment in time, energy, passion, and thoughtfulness.

VC PERSPECTIVE FROM THE FIELD:

THE STARK REALITY OF FORMING A VC FIRM

"Forming a VC firm is a long-term undertaking, unlike taking a job at Google or Facebook that you can leave in a year or two to do something else. Especially if you plan to do early-stage investing, the first close of your first fund brings a commitment of six to eight years of your life . . . and probably more. Because many first-time fund managers are not yet 35 years old, many have never stayed at one job for even five years. But in VC, each fund is set up as a 10-year commitment to investing. The expectation is to spend 10 years calling the capital into the fund, finding the suitable investments required to deploy the capital, helping to nurture the companies, helping these same companies raise subsequent capital, and ultimately achieving liquidity through an IPO or a trade sale. If things don't go well, you will find it's not nearly as painful to lose your own money as it is to lose your investors'. You probably will be inclined to do everything you can for as long as you can to produce as much success as you can. So, before you dive into the fundraising process of your first fund, make sure you are ready to commit a substantial portion of your career to the task!"

Know Your Value

Do you have a strong value proposition, track record of success, network, or skill set that is valuable for investing into and building companies?

Limited partners look for characteristics that make a fund valuable. They think about how you will invest, create value, and make them money. They will evaluate your individual merits and successes. They will also weigh your proposal relative to other funds with similar investment strategies and against current portfolios of their venture capital funds. When you pitch LPs, you must make the case for why they should invest in your fund. Understanding what LPs look for when evaluating venture capital funds will increase the odds of your success.

Understand When The Right Time Is

When is the right time to start a new firm and raise a venture capital fund?

Market timing plays a role, but raising a venture capital fund should be more about the right time for you, the venture capitalist, than the right time for the market.

How should you evaluate your readiness and positioning?

An aspiring venture capitalist should ask the challenging, introspective questions that characterize a rational investor who is fit to manage other people's capital, such as:

- Am I ready to take on the large responsibility of setting up a firm, raising capital, and investing in a portfolio of companies?

- What are my strengths as a venture capitalist?

- What do I bring to the table that others do not?

- What is my network?

- Do I have the ability to analyze companies and understand why they will be valuable?

- Can I get access to companies that have great teams?

- Do I have enough experience and confidence to source, pick, and win deals?

- Do I have the social capital, charisma, and vision to recruit a team and build a firm?

- Have I earned a respected reputation in the field that will allow me to partner with great company builders?

Take some time now as an active reader and answer those questions in your head or in a notebook. Be thorough and honest in answering the questions.

Form The Team

Should you embark on this journey as a lone venture capitalist or as a band of venture capitalist musketeers?

The team's composition is critically important given that LPs invest in people. First, think about who you would want to work with long term. Venture capital firms can fall apart if the team falls apart, not just because performance wanes. Prior work or investing experience with an individual or individuals can give you greater insight into whether you will work well together and have complementary goals.

Also think about what would produce higher returns: being a single venture capitalist or forming a team. Both have benefits and drawbacks. For example, working alone enables you to make decisions faster and move more quickly, creates less overhead for your firm, and allows you to strategize based on your own understanding of the market. With a partner or a team, there is more discussion from partners that are economic owners in the outcome of the fund, so they care more about the quality of the investments that make it into the portfolio and building the firm.

This can augment the investment diligence process but can also distract you through personality incompatibilities, communication challenges, and differences in philosophy or values. There is no right team size, even though many funds that aspire to be "the next Benchmark" expect to have somewhere between four and six partners when the firm is at maturity, or "the next Sequoia" where the firm reaches significant scale in assets under management (AUM) and is regarded as the top brand and investor in venture capital.

The team can determine how attractive LPs find your fund. For example, some LPs will not invest in funds run by a single venture capitalist. They view a single person running a venture fund as being too risky, even though some of the best-returning venture funds, especially at the smaller fund size, have been single venture capitalist funds.

VC PERSPECTIVE FROM THE FIELD:
HOW TO BUILD YOUR TEAM AND ADD A VC PARTNER

"Spend A LOT of time together, including outside of work. My partner and I met with countless founders and made several investments together before she officially joined. We commuted to the city together several days each week—about an hour each direction—giving us an opportunity to discuss companies, ideas, changes we wanted to make, events we hosted and went to—basically time to discuss everything. We also got together outside of work for family dinners, trips to the beach, kids' birthdays, Thanksgiving, etc. It was a great way to get to know each other personally.

Hire a CEO coach. We went through a deep personality assessment together, employing an experienced CEO coach. We then walked through the assessment in an in-depth session with the coach to figure out how we were similar and how we viewed our differences. This provided a common framework within which to understand the other person's behavior, a means of understanding, supporting, and pushing each other when needed.

Write a memo detailing the firm you want to build together. I recommend that you spend some time working with your prospective partner(s) to develop a vision for what you want the firm to be—what the pitch to entrepreneurs will be, the size of the fund, stage, focus, investment strategy, and the like. I recommend that you develop these independently as this is a good test on how closely aligned you are on your long-term vision and goals.

Talk candidly about numbers. Anyone who joins the firm should elevate the firm to such a degree that all are excited to share. But once you start to talk numbers, that is when things often get real. During this phase of the negotiation, I recommend that you focus on how the prospective partner negotiates, what he or she values, if lines are drawn in the sand, and where his/her focus lies. It's very telling and a good indication of priorities and values—not just how they'll behave as a partner, but also how they will work with founders."

Fund Size

Does the size of the fund matter?

The business model for a venture capitalist includes getting paid with management fees and later with a percentage of the profits when the companies sell or list publicly on a stock exchange. Why is this important? Well, in terms of management fees, if you charge 2 percent and raise $1 million dollars, you will receive a salary of only $20,000 before taxes, which may not be sustainable. While you are not a genie who can rub a magic lamp and raise a fund sufficient to cover expected costs, you should think about how to "right size" the fund to cover its operating budget, including building a team that fits your strategy and covering your cost of living. Some venture capitalists managing small funds allocate most of the fees from the first fund to build the firm and execute their strategies rather than taking a larger salary. Of course, foregoing a salary is a luxury for most. That is why you typically see individuals who already have a level of wealth entering venture capital: their day-to-day expenses are already covered. As you think about fund size, consider all your business expenses and remember to fairly compensate yourself. This is important for long-term success.

Determine Strategy

Which fundraising strategy is the best to use?

Part of deciding to raise a venture capital fund is creating an investment strategy that fits your background, that is executable, and that is repeatable. There are a few questions you should consider. You may again want to pause and answer these questions before you continue reading.

- What advantage do you have that you can articulate, is believable, and will help LPs clearly understand the value of your strategy?

- For example:

    ○ Do you have a great relationship with many founders in a network that have high potential to build large businesses?

    ○ Are you known as an experienced investor who can augment and complement the skillset of a technical founder?

    ○ Are you a thought leader with specialized industry knowledge that will enable you to persuade entrepreneurs to take your money?

    ○ Do you have an area advantage for sourcing?

- What resources do you need to execute your strategy, including other team members?

- What market forces could change over the course of the fund that would affect your strategy?

A strategy is hard to create and most first-time funds miss the mark and have to adjust. In today's market, there are some misconceptions as to what an investment strategy is. Some venture capitalists are too broad with their definition of strategy. A strategy is realizing that there is a gap or problem in the market and understanding how to fill this gap or solve this problem in a creative way that will win competitive deals. Some of the most experienced venture capitalists raising first-time funds tell investors they can find and invest in great entrepreneurs because they have an established network of great company builders, or because they have a reputation for building great companies. Younger entrepreneurs may seek out these experienced venture capitalists for capital and advice. You must deliberate, brainstorm, collect feedback, and test whether your own investment strategy is logical, reasonable, and in demand by investors. Conduct customer research. It is worth your time to iterate your strategy. Make sure it works and can be repeated.

VC PERSPECTIVE FROM THE FIELD:
WHAT TO KEEP IN MIND AT THE OUTSET OF FUNDRAISING

"The most important advice that can be given to those thinking of starting a new fund is to be thoughtful and prescriptive in building a firm that is sustainable and designed to succeed. Start with the end in mind. By doing so, you start with a vision of your ultimate impact and work backwards tactically to build a firm that will achieve that goal while staying true to your values and principles."

CHAPTER 2

Designing Your Fund's Investment Strategy

Strategy is about setting yourself apart from the competition. It's not a matter of being better at what you do—it's a matter of being different at what you do.

—Michael Porter

Every venture capitalist has to have an investment strategy, a plan that captures or creates value for investors. What constitutes a good investment strategy? First, it must make sense for the venture capitalist and the team at the helm. Secondly, the venture capitalist and her/his strategy must blend well like peas and carrots but also stand out.

Why A Limited Partner Should Choose Your Strategy

What are your unique insights and unfair advantages?

Limited partners look for an answer to the question, "Why you?" What makes you distinctive when you appear amidst a crowd of other venture capitalists, all wearing matching front-zip fleece vests? Do you have a key market insight that will lead to capturing a lot of value in a particular industry? Do you understand how blockchain really works? Do you have access to a great network of entrepreneurs who are great at building valuable businesses quickly? Did you ever lead an infrastructure technology team serving over a billion consumers at Facebook? Have you ever invested in dozens of the best Silicon Valley companies as an angel investor? Are you spinning out of one of the best venture capital firms in the world?

It is important to define an investment strategy that is authentic to your experience and skillset.

If the investment strategy doesn't relate to your past experience, then LPs will probably not feel compelled to commit to your fund. The limited partner needs to know what makes you different and whether you can capitalize on that difference.

Suppose you invest in Series A investments. For those unfamiliar with Series A, it is a financing round very early in a company's life cycle when the company is just starting to grow the team and generate revenue. Let's say that you have a track record of investing in Series A investments at a large, well-known, established venture capital firm, so you know what to look for when making an investment into a startup.

Then, you decide to branch out to raise your own fund with a strategy of continuing to invest in Series A investments. In this scenario, LPs may believe you will continue to be good at investing in great Series A investments.

However, if you decide to raise a fund that targets later-stage investments—such as the round before an initial public offering, when the team is in place and the company is generating consistently larger revenues—rather than in Series A investments, the limited partner will probably question your switch in focus. The limited partner may not believe you can execute your strategy because it is so different from previous strategies. This would require a transparent explanation to support the change and why you believe you would have an advantage executing a new investment strategy.

How Will You Make Money?

The venture capitalist must persuade the limited partner that the strategy can create value. Some questions the limited partner will ask when assessing the strategy include:

- Why is your investment strategy defensible, durable, and repeatable?

- What is the competitive edge that gives this venture capitalist an advantage over other venture capitalists to source, pick, and win the best venture capital deals?

- Why is this VC the right person to execute the fund strategy?

There is no simple answer as to what makes a good investment strategy because no one size fits all. Limited partners will invest in private fund strategies if they believe the strategies will create value and returns on invested capital. Having a different investment strategy may be an advantage. A new strategy offers the LPs something fresh to add to their portfolio. However, don't dismiss a strategy similar to strategies the limited partner has seen before. Familiarity has its advantages, particularly when there is an established team network, track record, and other factors.

What Is The Market (Growth) Opportunity?

Limited partners choose investment teams and thus, while the market growth potential of the investment strategy is important, it is usually less important than the team and its track record. Limited partners may be interested in venture capital funds that employ a generalist strategy, meaning the fund will invest in different sectors and business models in the same fund. Or they may invest in venture capital funds that employ a specialist strategy, investing in a single sector (e.g., automotive), geography (e.g., London), technology (e.g., blockchain), or network (e.g., YCombinator). There is no hard and fast rule for how Limited Partners think about which is best.

Of course, markets go up and down, changing over time, so the limited partner will weigh each fund investment in the context of market opportunity. If you are employing a generalist strategy, make sure to emphasize how you can be successful across multiple sectors. If employing a specialized strategy, be sure to have the requisite data and support to convince LPs that there is a large growth opportunity in the target market, and that enough valuable companies are being built in that market to make the investment opportunity attractive.

What is the value creation opportunity?

This means that within the market opportunity, you need to have a strategy to capture or create value. This ensures the ability to fund future investments. It is also important because it affects the limited partner's perception of the venture capitalist's involvement in devising a strategy for value creation. Investing is not the hard part. The hard part is translating those dollars into profit. Every aspect of the investment must produce value by increasing the worth of the investment. The limited partner needs to know if and when the venture capitalist discovers a problem or gap in the market and whether the venture capitalist is positioned to capture or create this value.

What is your deal flow?

A big part of being successful as a venture capitalist is your deal flow. Therefore, you should have a good grasp of how you will source deals for your fund. There are many ways to source good companies; the key is making sure you position yourself to see all the top investment opportunities, giving you a chance to review and invest in those opportunities.

Before investing, LPs will want to understand your deal flow, particularly where and how you are seeing the best companies. While this would seem obvious, it is often overlooked by emerging managers. They should be able to go into detail about their networks and how they source good deals.

For example, perhaps you are a thesis-driven investor, meaning you develop a thesis about an investment opportunity and then seek investment opportunities.

Or, perhaps you are more reactionary in sourcing, building a personal reputation and brand that attracts founders and CEOs.

No matter where your deal flow comes from, you should think about access. How much capital can you realistically invest in these companies? Another consideration is selection—how do you ensure you invest in the best mouse trap from among the 20 companies building mouse traps?

Setting Your Values And What You Stand For

What is important?

As an investor, you should know your values and what you stand for. What are your beliefs? What is important to you? How will you run your firm? How will you treat other people at your firm, including partners and junior staff? How will you treat entrepreneurs and other people you interact with? Why would entrepreneurs want to work with you?

As a venture capitalist, you may have the necessary experience to help grow businesses, but your reputation as a fundamentally good person to work with can make or break a deal with a limited partner. The LP will undoubtedly interact with others in the VC ecosystem and will hear how you are to deal with. They are searching for investors with good values who will be great partners for the long term.

That is, if your investment strategy needs to evolve, are you a chameleon or a horseshoe crab? Can you be disciplined as well as flexible and adaptable?

Imagine you start with a strategy that takes advantage of a market dislocation, but the strategy becomes less relevant over the course of your fund. Can you change with your surroundings like a chameleon? When your investment strategy no longer works or is overrun by competition, can you adapt the strategy?

Or are you a horseshoe crab, a creature that has effectively stopped evolving because it has already found a competitive advantage in the biological landscape?
In this case, perhaps you have an enduring strategy, one flexible enough to adapt
through market changes. For example, a strategy focused on data-oriented companies is probably sufficiently broad enough to source great investments to
endure over market cycles.

As you can see, neither the chameleon nor the horseshoe crab is better than the
other. They both have advantages and disadvantages. Most venture capitalists
strive for balance but lean towards one or the other. When you think about your
fund's investment strategy and how it evolves vis-à-vis, these two creatures can
help shape a strategy that is effective over time. Be aware, however, of the concept of "strategy drift" or "style drift," terms coined by LPs to describe a venture
capitalist who drifts too far from the original strategy. This concerns LPs because
they invested in one strategy but now have exposure to another one. They may
question your experience and ability to produce returns in using that strategy.

Can you dare to be different?

When setting your investment strategy, be bold, but consider all possibilities.
Will you be the first person to use data science to create an advantage for sourcing and picking investments? Will you be the first person who invests in seed
stage companies? Daring to be different is a good way to position your fund, but
avoid the extreme. For example, if you are the first fund to raise all of your capital commitments with cryptocurrencies, you may have a hard time getting
institutional LPs on board.

Being too different can be perceived as posing a higher risk, but that does not
necessarily mean it is wrong. Limited partners are effectively paying you—the
subject matter expert—to find and take advantage of gaps in the market. Make
sure you create a strategy that makes you different, creates value, and is executable.

Fund Size And Portfolio Construction

How do you define fund size?

As a first-time fund, you may not have much choice about fund size. It is rare with a first-time fund to easily raise the targeted fund size. That said, fund size is a function of your strategy and should enable you to execute that strategy, building a portfolio with enough ownership of each private company to generate returns at the fund level. The concept most closely associated with the right fund size is portfolio construction.

What is portfolio construction?

Portfolio construction refers to the relationship between fund size, the number of investments in the portfolio, and the capital invested in each company. As a venture capitalist, you should take a step back and think: when the fund is fully invested, what will the portfolio look like? How many companies will be in the portfolio? How much capital will be invested in each company initially, but also over time as you invest capital again into the same company in what is called a follow-on investment? Having the end in mind when thinking about portfolio construction will help you manage returns at the fund level.

Given that dollars are returned to LPs at the fund level, this is an important topic for them, and it is one they want venture capitalists to understand. Limited partners do not want to commit dollars only to learn later that the venture capitalist has not gotten enough ownership in each company, or that he/she has not reserved enough capital to protect ownership in their best companies, causing returns to suffer at the fund level.

Another way to think about portfolio construction is the following: how do I ensure I am optimizing my chances of success at the fund level while maximizing the potential value creation?

Now that the strategy is set, get into the market and begin executing your strategy. Invest in companies that are a practical fit. This will allow LPs to see that you follow through on what you say. Action is powerful when convincing LPs that you are the right venture capitalist for their portfolio.

CHAPTER 3

Plan And Prepare Your Fundraising Materials

A good plan now is better than a great plan too late.

—Verne Harnish

Introduction

You have decided to raise a venture capital fund. It is now time to bring that vision to life and organize your ideas by preparing fundraising materials and designing a plan. The following outline and questions will help you get started. Do not get discouraged, though, if everything does not go as planned during the fundraising process.

Raising a venture capital fund is a sales process. You are selling a financial security that is a stake in the fund. Whether you have one limited partner or a hundred, you must be able to sell your vision. This means persuading LPs you are the right investor to achieve high returns for their investment portfolio.

It is challenging to raise a venture capital fund. Many who start out do not actually get to the finish line. There are several reasons why this happens. The aspiring venture capitalist may have ambition, but not yet have a strong enough network from which to raise capital. Fund size targets are set for how much to raise, but they may fall short of a first close because LP do not get behind it.

Often the limited partner never discloses the reason for the pass. Some are highly risk averse and will rarely invest in new fund managers, particularly first-time fund managers who are just beginning to build their firms.

In other cases, the venture capital fund may not fit into a limited partner's investment strategy. Or a limited partner may write checks too big for the fund size. The limited partner may not have enough capital left to invest in new funds and opt to invest almost exclusively in his/her existing portfolio. This process is known as the "re-up" or "re-upping with existing managers." Finally, the LPs may just not be interested in what you are offering.

If you find during the process that you do not fit in well with a given limited partner, do not be discouraged. Instead, be encouraged that you were able to begin a relationship with this limited partner. He or she may invest in your fund at some point down the road or may invest directly in some of your portfolio companies.

She/he could also introduce you to other LPs who are more risk seeking or who can offer feedback on your pitch to make it more compelling. When a limited partner opts not to invest, move on with your process and engage other LPs.

Remember, a pass on your fund is not an absolute no. Quite the contrary. Limited partners can always change their minds, even in the same fundraising cycle—indeed, even on the same day. A personal example of this was when an investment partner made a unilateral decision that resulted in saying, "Thanks, but no thanks" to a venture capitalist. Later that day, after a short discussion with his team, the partner decided to reverse that decision. An email was sent to the venture capitalist saying, "By the way, we are ready to kick off diligence if you would have us!" The probability of all this happening on the same day is slim, but it does happen. So, act accordingly during the diligence process and consider any "no" as a maybe.

Once you have caught the attention of the limited partner, you want to keep it. Be sure to update LPs on all progress. Keep them apprised of developments such as new investments made since the last meeting or any additions to or subtractions from the team. Notify them of any changes in the timing of the process. If fundraising is going well and you believe you are going to close the fund sooner than expected, let the LPs know. This gives them an opportunity to rearrange their own calendars to prioritize your funds.

Necessary Documents To Have During Fundraising

What is a pitch deck?

A pitch deck[7] is a series of slides created by the venture capitalist that is shared with LPs. Some pitch decks by top-tier funds don't have to make a strong investment case and are fewer than ten pages. Others are more than fifty pages long because the venture capitalist needs to elaborate on what makes the strategy work or what makes the market opportunity attractive.

Most pitch decks range between ten and twenty pages with most about twenty pages long, especially if you have to go in-depth on a particular part of the investment strategy. There is no set length to a pitch deck, but there is something to be said for being concise.

A pitch deck encompasses all aspects of the fund investment opportunity, including team, strategy, prior performance (known as track record or partner attribution), and terms. The following questions are important and should be answered first: Who are you? What have you done well? What are you going to

---

[7] Technically, a pitch deck is not required to raise a venture capital fund, but realistically, every LP that will invest into the fund will need to understand what they are buying, and the pitch deck remains the best means to convey this information and narrative to date.

do to make money now? And why do you need to start another venture capital fund and exist in the market?

Other questions to consider include: What are your values? What is your strategy? How will you make money? How have you previously made money? What are the basic terms of the fund? These are fundamental questions that need to be answered in any pitch deck. The limited partner can then assess whether your fund opportunity is something worth reviewing.

Your answers should be succinct—don't expound on your investment banking or management consulting slide-building skills. But if you have a proprietary database or data science team, that gives you an advantage in sourcing deals, or if you are an area-specific fund and you need to explain why investing in Eastern Europe is highly attractive based on a risk-adjusted returns analysis, then perhaps these should make it into the pitch deck. Use only what is necessary to convey the point.

The pitch deck is the first impression, but not the only impression. You want it to be polished before sharing it with prospective LPs. You may even consider hiring a marketing or design firm to format your slides so they are relevant and stand out.

A good pitch deck resembles a good piece of art—it moves the viewer, it conveys necessary elements without including extraneous items, and it is influential. It should be one of the first documents sent to a limited partner and should include enough information for the limited partner to make a decision on whether to meet with you. It also allows the limited partner to contextualize your fund opportunity. Are you a seed fund? Are you a later-stage fund? Are you focused on the consumer? Are you focused on the enterprise? Both? Are you based in Europe? Israel? U.S.A.? A pitch deck should answer these questions.

You might have only thirty to sixty minutes to make your pitch, so time your pitch deck. But the pitch deck may not necessarily be presented during an in-person meeting. If you send a pitch deck to a limited partner in advance, she/he can read it and prepare for the meeting. In this case, be ready to expound on the pitch deck in conversation with the LP.

EXAMPLE OF OPEN-SOURCED PITCH DECK

Notation II Pitch Deck

https://www.slideshare.net/Notation/notation-ii-pitch-deck

For Notation II, Notation summarizes Fund I, addresses what they have learned, and provides a context for what has changed over the course of Fund I and in advance of Fund II. They also note that the strategy is shifting, albeit slightly, for the second fund. Being clear and concise like this deck is something to strive for in a pitch deck.

Some venture capitalists have multiple versions of their pitch deck. They may have an abbreviated version of the deck as a brief overview of the fund to send to LPs they do not know well. If the limited partner is interested, then the venture capitalist can send a lengthier version. Venture capitalists can adjust slides and highlight individual parts of the strategy to appeal to specific LPs. For example, you may have a different pitch for an endowment versus a family office, given a potential difference of what each LP wants from you when investing in your fund. You want to share enough material to inspire interest, but not so much as to overwhelm.

What is a Limited Partnership Agreement, also referred to as an LPA?

The Limited Partnership Agreement, or LPA, is a legal contract governing the relationship between the limited partner and the venture capitalist. The venture capitalist uses the LPA to form the venture capital fund, known as a Limited Partnership. The Limited Partnership Agreement exists because a venture capital fund is a partnership between the VC and LPs.

It defines the terms of the partnership, including names, addresses, purpose of the partnership, voting rights, how decisions are made, accounting and auditing information, how the economics are split between the VC and the LPs, how the partnership can be dissolved, as well as other terms that clarify how the fund works.

VCs and LPs both have goals when drafting a Limited Partnership Agreement. The venture capitalist wants the LPA to be a flexible document allowing him/her to change the strategy when necessary. The limited partner, on the other hand, wants stricter terms so he/she understands the parameters within which the venture capitalist will act. Limited partners depend on the performance of the venture capitalist in whom they are investing and try to get the right terms to protect their investment. The LPA therefore is used as a risk management tool for LPs.

What is a Summary of Terms?

Just as it sounds, the Summary of Terms is a succinct summary of the fund terms. Think of the Summary of Terms as an abbreviated version of the Limited Partnership Agreement. Rather than the limited partner having to read in detail through the Limited Partnership Agreement to understand key terms, you boil down the key terms into a short summary. Here is an example of a shorter summary of terms in a pitch deck:

- Target Fund Size
- Investment Term
- Management Fee
- Carried Interest

In this example, the target fund size is the size of the fund you would like to raise. The investment term is the length of time in which you can make new investments. The management fee is the fee you charge on committed capital. The carried interest, also known as carry or the incentive fee, is the fee you charge on the profits of the fund. For example, if the carried interest is twenty percent, and you make ten million in profits, your carried interest fee would be two million.

Here is an example of a longer summary of terms:

- Limited partnership name and legal entity location
- General partnership name and legal entity location
- Management company name and legal entity location
- Headquarters (where the General Partners are based)
- Target Fund Size
- Minimum LP Check Size
- Investment Period
- Fund Term
- Strategy
- Industry Focus
- Target Return
- Reserves for Follow-on
- GP Commitment
- Management Fee
- Preferred Return
- Carried Interest
- Fee Offsets
- Clawback
- Management Company Structure
- Investment Committee Members and Key Persons
- Reporting Requirements

How is the Limited Partnership Agreement used?

The Limited Partnership Agreement can be used to resolve disputes that could arise and determines the contractual relationship between the VC and LP.

When does a Limited Partnership Agreement fit into the due diligence process?

The LPA is negotiated in coordination with the attorneys for the venture capitalist and the limited partner. The process is iterative, meaning that the venture capitalist and the limited partner will sometimes go through multiple rounds of negotiations before the LPA is finished. Limited partners investing the most amount of money have the greatest influence over the final version of the agreement. This does not eliminate the influence of LPs investing less money because they can still provide feedback.

The venture capitalist does not have to accept any of the feedback but instead can set his/her own terms. These terms may be unacceptable to the LPs, possibly causing them to withdraw from the investment. However, because the relationship between a VC and an LP is built on trust and respect, probably the negotiations will end in agreement, with both sides giving and taking during the negotiation.

Who negotiates the Limited Partnership Agreement during the due diligence process?

There are four parties typically involved in LPA discussions: the limited partner, the lawyer of the limited partner, the venture capitalist, and his/her lawyer.

How is the Limited Partnership Agreement drafted?

The LPA is written initially by the venture capitalists and their lawyer. If you are working with an experienced fund formation lawyer, the lawyer will typically know the market terms that could be offered to LPs. The lawyer may also have an LPA with standard language to use as a template, so you are not drafting an LPA from scratch.

Once drafted, the LPA is sent to the LPs, who then review it with their lawyers. This process is referred to as the LPA comments period, during which LPs can comment on the LPA and return those comments to the venture capitalist. The venture capitalist is not obligated to change the LPA based on the comments, although it helps to set the tone for a future partnership between them.

Drafting an LPA can take a few weeks, or it can take up to a few months to conclude negotiations between the venture capitalist and the limited partner. An average Limited Partnership Agreement is between fifty and one hundred and fifty pages.

It is important to note that there are two distinct limited partner comment periods. The first comment period includes LPs very close to the VC, especially the influential early-investor LPs, who have strong opinions or who will be instrumental in helping the venture capitalist's fundraising effort. This can be an insular part of the process that results in a select group of LPs having the majority of influence over terms set in the LPA. All other LPs who commit to the fund after this initial comment period usually do not have as much influence over the terms unless they bring something very special to the VC, such as a large commitment check. This split of the comment period pertains to funds that work with anchor LPs or funds having a first close with an institutional limited partner.

When the document is complete and no more changes will be made, the final draft is circulated to all the LPs.

Why is the Limited Partnership Agreement important?

The LPA terms are what governs the venture capital fund. It codifies the terms of the venture capital fund, which can only be changed through a side letter. The side letter is a separate legal contract giving rights to different LPs outside of the LPA or through an amendment to the LPA. This amendment is agreed upon by the venture capitalist and limited partner and changes the meaning of a previously agreed upon term.

How do you form the Limited Partnership Agreement?

The first step in forming an LPA is to talk to a fund formation lawyer. There are many law firms that can help you. The goal is to talk with a fund formation lawyer who has helped form similar firms. For example, if there is a law firm that has worked with seed stage venture firms, it may serve you better to work with this law firm as they will be more familiar with the terms requisite for your fund type. The same goes for venture capital funds that may have non-traditional structures. Go to a law firm or lawyer experienced in working with your structure and in your fund.

What are the terms found in a typical Limited Partnership Agreement?

The Limited Partnership Agreement, or LPA, is full of convoluted and sometimes obtusely written language. The legal terms contributing to the length of the document are necessary because they legally define how to resolve issues arising during the course of the venture capital fund's existence.

Given the complexity of the LPA, it is difficult to address all the possible terms, but I describe most commonly used terms below.

What are the common terms included in the Limited Partnership Agreement?

Formation of the Partnership and Naming of the Principal

This establishes the partnership, the names of the principals, and the main location where the business will operate.

Purpose of the Partnership

This defines the purpose of the partnership—that is, what the venture capitalist will do with the fund.

Term of the Partnership

This defines the length of the partnership and sets terms that could extend the duration of the venture capital fund if it becomes necessary to sell the remaining companies in the fund.

Accounting of the Partnership

This is an important section that defines many parts of how the venture capital fund will manage its accounting practices, including LP rights to access the accounting and tax information of the venture capital fund, or Limited Partners hip.

Capital Contributions

Terms relating to how the venture capitalist can "call" capital from the Limited Partners for the Limited Partners hip and other policies, such as taking on loans or withdrawing capital from the Limited Partners hip.

Profits and Losses

The profits and losses shared between the venture capitalist and limited partner.

Capital Accounts

A capital account held by the venture capitalist for the limited partner.

Net Cash Flow

The net cash flow distributed between the venture capitalist and limited partner, including the timing of those distributions.

Administrative Provisions

This involves a number of issues for the venture capitalist, such as management responsibilities, how much time is devoted to administrative work, limitations of liability and indemnification, limitations of liability for the limited partner, fees, and other authority assigned to the venture capitalist.

Death or Withdrawal of a Partner

This defines what happens when the venture capitalist becomes no longer active in the venture capital fund.

Transfer of Partnership Interest

Policies and restrictions concerning transfers of ownership in the Limited Partners hip. For example, if a limited partner wanted to sell his/her stake in the Limited Partners hip, this section defines how that process should happen.

Dissolution and Termination of the Partnership

The provisions defining scenarios for the closing down of a venture capital fund.

What are amendments to the Limited Partnership Agreement and when are they needed?

If the venture capitalist or limited partner wants to make a change to the LPA, the LPA can be amended. The amendment proposal is made by the venture capitalist or could originate from a limited partner's suggestion. The amendment is then voted. These voting rights are typically defined in (you guessed it!) the LPA.

In most cases, a majority or supermajority of the limited partner's support is needed to change the LPA. This protects the limited partner from the possibility that a venture capitalist will change the LPA on a whim. Many times, voting rights are defined by the dollars invested in the venture capital fund: the more dollars invested, the more weight the vote holds. If voting is run on majority and a limited partner has fifty-one percent of the fund's invested capital then, she/he could single-handedly push through changes to the LPA. This is worth thinking about when managing control of your fund.

Amendments are not very common, but when they do arise, they are circulated among the LPs by the VC before the formal vote. VCs spend time ensuring the LPs are comfortable with the amendment and with the reasoning behind the amendment. This is important for maintaining trust between the venture capitalist and limited partner.

What is the subscription agreement?

The subscription agreement is a legal document that is effectively an application to join the Limited Partners hip. It details the representations, warranties, and covenants of LPs investing in the venture capital fund.

In practice, subscription agreements are usually handled by the VC's and the LP's lawyers. These documents are largely a formality given the importance of the Limited Partnership Agreement, which ultimately governs the fund. It is important for the limited partner to submit these documents before the closing of the fund so he/she can be included legally.

The document is submitted by the limited partner, but the venture capitalist can decide to accept or deny it, even if the limited partner has gone through full diligence up to that point.

Why, after so many hours, days, and weeks of work, would the venture capitalist deny the subscription agreement application?

In rare cases, the venture capitalist may reject the limited partner's subscription documents and not allow him/her into the fund. No specific reason needs to be given by the venture capitalist, but it doesn't make a good impression on the limited partner, nor does it look good for the venture capitalist.

It is best to be transparent with your prospective LPs throughout the diligence process. If at some point, it does not make sense to move forward with one or more of them, let them know as soon as possible. If you choose not to move forward because you are over-subscribed, or for some other reason that you are not obligated to disclose, you should maintain the relationship because you could potentially become partners in a later fund.

"Nice-To-have" Documents to Have During Fundraising

What is an Executive Summary (or Teaser)?

The Executive Summary, or Teaser, is a shorter version of the pitch deck. It is only one or two pages and includes an explanation of the investment opportunity. Venture capitalists who are not yet comfortable with sharing all of the information in the pitch deck can send the Executive Summary in advance of a call or meeting with a limited partner. If there is a concern that your pitch deck will be shared with other LPs or potential competitors, then perhaps the Executive Summary is the right document to initially share.

The main sections of the Executive Summary could include:

- Name of your fund

- Overview of the fund

- Overview of investment strategy (make sure this is well-thought-out and different)

- Overview of the team

- Investment terms, including fund size, fees, and venture capitalist's commitment (optional)

What is a Private Placement Memorandum, or PPM?

The Private Placement Memorandum, or PPM, is a legal document prepared by you and your lawyer focused on the fund offering. It discloses a significant amount of information about the fund investment opportunity. The PPM is helpful to the venture capitalist when making decisions on the merits of the investment.

The main sections of the PPM include:

Summary of Investment Opportunity

This contains information such as the fund name, target fund size, and brief review of the strategy, process, and market opportunity. It can include information on the organization, the team, where the team is based, location of the fund, and target investment geography. It can also include distinctions that make the venture capital fund unique, as well as any history of the venture capital firm, including prior funds and performance.

Summary of Key Terms

This is an expanded version of the summary and key terms in the pitch deck. It simplifies the key terms defined in the LPA. In short, the limited partner should be able to look at this abbreviated summary of terms and quickly get a good idea of whether she/he can invest structurally or legally. For example, some investors may have legal restrictions on whether they can invest in certain jurisdictions outside of the United States. If you are raising a fund based outside of the U.S., this would be evident in the summary of terms, and the limited partner would quickly realize that this opportunity is not a fit. A few questions that LPs may consider when reading through the summary of terms are the following: How much are the fund fees? How long should the limited partner expect to have his/her capital locked up in the fund? How long will you be making new investments? How much are you committing yourself to the fund? Are you charging market rates for your fees?

Investment Performance

A detailed track record of the performance of the fund. Segmenting performance by fund is helpful for LPs. Other ways to segment the performance data could be by vintage year, by strategy, by geography, or by partner.

Organization

This includes a detailed review of the organization, including all team members, what their roles are, and their biographies.

Strategy

An overview of the investment strategy.

Process

An in depth look at the investment process, including deal sourcing, diligence, selecting, and working with the companies after investment.

Market Opportunity

A comprehensive review of the market opportunities, including any relevant sector strategies, such as real estate or agricultural technology.

Case Studies

If you have prior investments, this section could be used to highlight the investment thesis and other pertinent details so the limited partner gets a good sense of what types of companies you invest in, at what stage you get involved with these companies, and how they have performed post-investment.

Investment Considerations and Risk Factors

This section should be written with your lawyer.

Potential Conflicts of Interest

Write this one with your lawyer too.

Legal, Regulatory and Tax Matters

Again, write this section with your lawyer!

What is a Due Diligence Questionnaire (DDQ)?

The Due Diligence Questionnaire, or DDQ, highlights the most frequently asked questions by LPs. As a VC, you will find that potential partners ask similar questions. Rather than repeating yourself, a DDQ provides the answers, and the limited partner can review them at her/his convenience.

You don't need to reinvent the wheel because the industry organization known as the Institutional Limited Partners Association (ILPA) maintains a comprehensive DDQ on its website:

https://ilpa.org/due-diligence-questionnaire/

ILPA's due diligence questionnaire is more comprehensive than you would normally need as a venture capitalist or care to receive and read as an LP, so I would recommend adapting this DDQ so it answers the questions necessary for LPs who would invest in the fund.

What is an Operating Manual?

Many VC firms do not create operating manuals. Though an operating manual is a rare production by a venture capital firm, some venture capitalists still choose to create them. An operating manual is a formal document venture capitalists and employees of the venture capital firm use to help them perform their functions correctly and efficiently. Operating manuals are used more often as a transparent form of marketing. Transparency is valued more by entrepreneurs, and venture capitalists want to show themselves to be aligned with the entrepreneurs' values.

If venture capitalists share what they believe in and how they work in an operating manual, some entrepreneurs may recognize the alignment of values and work ethic and decide to work with the venture capitalist. Some of these forms are now posted online, such as GitHub, a software development platform. Here are two examples used of seed firms Bloomberg Beta and Notation Capital using an operating manual.

Bloomberg Beta:

https://github.com/Bloomberg-Beta/Manual/blob/master/1%20-%20Manual.md

Notation Capital:

https://github.com/NotationCapital/Operating-Manual

What is the manifesto?

A manifesto written by a venture capitalist is a marketing document explaining the reasons why a venture capitalist exists and his/her views on investing. It is similar to an operating manual, though the manifesto will most likely have less information about the investment process and other internal fund activities.

Manifestos, sometimes called mantras, are not very popular, but some venture capitalists choose to write them. The term manifesto conjures up a revolutionary espousing an ideology, but a manifesto can also serve as a public document to declare intentions and motives for why your fund exists. These can include an investment thesis you find attractive or how you will take advantage of an evolving economy. It might offer insight into how the status quo of investing will change and why you are prepared to take advantage of that change.

Given that LPs like to ask why your new fund should be formed when a number of other funds already exist, this could be one way to give them answers.

A manifesto is not necessary, but it is a way to attract people aligned with your mission, goals, and beliefs. The manifesto is used less as a fundraising document and is posted publicly on the venture capitalist's website.

Here are a few examples of fund manifestos:

Founders Fund

https://foundersfund.com/the-future/

Ribbit Capital

https://ribbitcap.com/our-mantra/

CRV

https://www.crv.com/manifesto/

A manifesto is different from thesis-driven investing or thematic investing. A thesis and a theme, while similar, are too different. A thesis is a set of beliefs the venture capitalist has that focus on why and how his/her investments will become successful. It requires being thoughtful, making predictions, and running each investment through a set of predetermined criteria before investing. A thesis-driven strategy must be maintained and validated over time.

An example of a thesis-driven firm is Union Square Ventures, based in New York City.

Here is the USV thesis example as it changes over time:

Thesis 1.0

https://www.usv.com/blog/investment-thesis-usv

Thesis 2.0

https://www.usv.com/blog/usv-thesis-20

Thesis 3.0

https://www.usv.com/blog/usv-thesis-30

Thematic investing is also different from a manifesto. Thematic investing is basically investing in general ideas versus thesis-driven investing. Thematic investing picks a theme—say financial services or healthcare—and is a top-down analysis. It wants to figure out what to invest in and is more general than thesis-driven investing.

An example of a thematic investing firm is Foundry Group, which invests in general themes within technology that they believe are pervasive, relevant, and important.

The Data Room

What is the data room?

A data room is a secure online service that a venture capitalist uses to assemble digital copies of fundraising materials to share with the limited partner. While some venture capitalist funds still use physical data rooms, with fundraising materials printed on paper that LPs can access during a dedicated diligence session, this process is rather outdated. It is used only when there is a highly sensitive internal document that the venture capitalist will show when the limited partner visits the venture capitalist. To give you a sense of how uncommon they are today, in the hundreds of due diligence processes I have conducted on funds in the last decade, I have seen fewer than five physical data rooms.

An electronic data room is accessible in real-time by all LPs once the venture capitalist decides to share the data room with him/her. The key to a good data room is that it is secure and user-friendly. It can also be shared easily with colleagues and should maintain the confidentiality of the fundraising materials in the data room. Access to the data room is allowed only after the venture capitalist has established a connection with the limited partner, and the limited partner has expressed interest in investing. The limited partner will then be provided with a username, password, and login instructions.

What are the advantages of the data room?

An electronic data room is a robust tool that allows you to administer who sees what and when. This real-time access allows a single person to manage effectively which fundraising materials have been shared and with whom. This real-time access to a data room means the venture capitalist can immediately share the data room with as many LPs as they wish to conduct due diligence. Having a centralized location for sharing fundraising materials with a limited partner allows several members of the limited partner team across different areas to work on the VC investment as well.

A data room is a useful way to engage transparently and with many existing and prospective LPs. By having a data room, the LPs will be able to find answers to many questions about the fund and why they should invest. A data room should give the limited partner ample opportunity to work through the process of assessing the fund as an investment opportunity and making a decision on whether to invest.

What are the advantages of an electronic data room?

There are three big advantages to an electronic data room: saving time, saving money, and having real-time access. If information requested by the limited partner is provided in advance, it enables him/her to do the research and diligence needed to become comfortable with making an investment.

The data room saves money by eliminating the need to hire additional people to manage the fundraising process, or to manage all of the interactions with the limited partner. Keeping resources lean can save you money on tedious processes and petty tasks that just cost employee time.

Perhaps the limited partner does not have a great internal system for sharing materials across teams. A data room could solve this challenge. Being able to share electronic materials is especially helpful when looking for information to support an investment committee's investment proposal, which is prepared by institutional LPs to obtain investment committee approval to invest in a venture capital fund.

Dealing with confidential fundraising documents can be stressful. Being able to share specific fundraising materials throughout the process on an as-needed basis is advantageous for the venture capitalist. This process is referred to as permissioning. Having an electronic data room also allows venture capitalists to monitor how active LPs are in their diligence process. For example, the venture capitalist can see how many times LPs have opened fundraising documents. This enables the venture capitalist to follow-up appropriately with both the most active LPs, who are engaged, and the less active LPs, who may need a reminder to keep reviewing the investment opportunity.

What are good data room models?

Data rooms should be user-friendly and have features needed to easily share documents with LPs. There are service providers for this purpose who sell licenses to use their data rooms. Before buying a license, however, read the reviews.

IntraLinks, Docsend, Google Drive, Box, and Dropbox are common data room service providers. There should be one data room to use by both the VC and LP throughout the fundraising process. If a third party manages the data room, be diligent about security measures and be aware of customer service in case there are any technical difficulties that arise during the fundraising process.

Choose a third-party service carefully. What the service provides can be important. For example, if a limited partner cannot copy, download, or print any files, this may not be a good thing. You may lose points with the LP for making life more difficult in terms of getting the information and sharing it with teammates, including members of the investment committee that are required to see information.

How do you organize the data room by folder hierarchy?

Organize the data room so it is easy to use. If you enjoy creating folder hierarchies, then this exercise is for you! One way of organizing folders is as follows:

- Fundraising Materials
    - Executive Summary
    - Pitch Deck
- Organization
    - Biographies
    - Organization Chart
- Track Record
    - Track Record (for each VC and current team combined)
- Legal
    - Summary of Terms
    - Limited Partnership Agreement (Word and PDF)
    - Limited Partnership Agreement, redlined (Word)

- Operational Due Diligence

  ○ Private Placement Memorandum

  ○ Due Diligence Questionnaire

  ○ List of major service providers, including Fund Administrator, Outsourced Chief Financial Officer, Compliance, Bank or Custodian, Tax Advisor

- References

  ○ Reference list for each venture capitalist

What other fundraising materials should be included?

In addition to the main categories above, there are other fundraising materials developed at a venture capitalist firm that are useful for the limited partner in determining whether to make a commitment. These include:

Code of Ethics

This is a set of guidelines published by venture capitalists that helps employees act in accordance with good values and ethical behavior.

Investment Memos and/or Investment Case Studies

If the venture capitalist has previously invested, it is helpful for the limited partner to understand why the venture capitalist chose those investments, as well as details of the transactions. The limited partner can then better understand the venture capitalist's investment strategy and how he/she has invested historically. Sometimes investment case studies are shared, including information about the performance of the company post-investment, including any significant value added by the venture capitalist.

Cash Flow Financial Statements

These are included when the venture capitalist already has at least one fund that has been active for a couple of years. These documents can help LPs assess the deployment pace of the venture capitalist as well as expected cash timing of returns.

Past Quarterly Financial Statements

If the venture capitalist has already been investing, then quarterly financial statements previously provided to LPs should be disclosed.

Past Year-end Audited Financial Statement

This is the audited version of the quarterly financial statements. This is always the fourth-quarter financial statement, ending at year end or December 31st. This quarterly statement is performed once a year and conducted by an outside third-party auditor that confirms that financial information disclosed by the venture capitalist. For institutional LPs, these audited financial statements are very important.

Past AGM Materials

This can be extraneous, but if you have spent the time preparing materials for past annual general meetings, and you are comfortable sharing them with LPs, then continue the practice.

Legal Entity Chart

Include a chart that shows the legal structure of the fund. This is especially useful if you are setting up your fund outside the United States.

Environmental, Social, and Governance (ESG) Policy

While this may be extraneous, these documents are becoming more useful. If you have spent the time drafting an ESG policy, especially if you are a mission-oriented venture capital firm, it would make sense to include this document.

Disaster Recovery Plan

The disaster recovery plan is a documented process or set of procedures to be executed by the venture capitalist to recover the technical infrastructure of the venture capital fund in the event of a disaster.

Compliance Manual

This technical document includes various internal policies, including personal trading, internal compliance, confidentiality, and training.

Carried Interest Calculation

It can be helpful to include an Excel sheet that shows an example of the carried interest calculation. This may be requested by the limited partner during the operational due diligence and is helpful for his/her accounting team, which may be trying to understand and forecast future cash flows.

Management Company Budget

The management company budget enables the LPs to see that the venture capitalist has thought about the fund as an operating business and also to get a better understanding of how fees will be spent over the course of the fund.

Market Research

After significant research has been completed on issues related to your investment strategy, include this research in the data room. It is especially helpful for area-focused funds or industry-specialized funds, such as healthcare or financial services.

The Manifesto

If you have written a manifesto, share it with

When is the time to share the data room with limited ͫ

Share the data room after a limited partner request. Usually this happens aɪ
the first or second meeting. A compelling investment proposal will prompt the
limited partner to request to see your data room to further explore the investment opportunity. You can share everything or be selective with the materials.
If you are hesitant to share the data room with prospective LPs, figure out why.
Are there deeper reasons to be concerned? What are they?

To give an example of how you might interact with a limited partner before
sharing a data room, here is a series of normal events:

1. A close mutual acquaintance makes you aware of a potential limited
    partner via e-mail.

2. Thank your mutual acquaintance and BBC her/him asking when it
    would be a good time to reach out to the prospective limited partner
    by phone or in person for a thirty-minute introductory call.

3. The limited partner will respond. Probably the limited partner CC's an
    assistant to set up a meeting. At this time, the limited partner may ask
    you to send any fundraising materials you are comfortable sharing.

4. You should send the executive summary or pitch deck at this time to
    the limited partner so it can be reviewed before the meeting. Also send
    a calendar invite to the limited partner and be clear about who will be
    invited on your calendar. A phone number is almost always included.
    If multiple people are to attend, then use a conference line; if only one
    person, directly dial this person.

5. After a successful meeting with the limited partner, a request is often
    made to access the data room. If all materials are prepared, you can

disclose the full data room with the LPA, sub docs, and all other supporting materials.

How should you track data room usage?

You can keep track of sharing your data room via the CRM you use for the fundraising process. There are several online data room software providers that will organize who you shared your data room with. These online providers will also show you when LPs enter the data room, what they looked at, and how much time they spent in each of the documents.

How much information should be shared?

A data room provides the venture capitalist with the ability to control when documents are shared with the limited partner. Sometimes it makes sense to withhold certain information for disclosure in another part of the process. For instance, legal documents and the limited partner Agreement take longer for lawyers to prepare and are usually requested by LPs later in the process, so it's not necessary for the VC to share the LPA immediately. Sharing information is at the discretion of the venture capitalist.

What do LPs do with the data?

The limited partner will use the data room for diligence on your fund. The limited partner may also look at similar investment opportunities and use the data room to compare your funds to other investment opportunities. One responsibility of the limited partner is to be aware of who is raising which funds. Another is to know what opportunities provide attractive investments. Limited partners might want to access your data room to get information for these reasons. Before allowing access to the data room, be sure that the LPs intention is to invest in your fund and not just to gather information. Knowing the background and reputation of the LPs will help determine their motives for viewing the data room.

Analyses can vary widely by LPs. Some LPs will perform quantitative due diligence; others may never perform any additional quantitative analyses beyond what you give them. As a best practice, aim to provide the limited partner with performance data that enables a thorough investment strategy review. If this is a first-time fund with a limited track record, then there may not be much data. On the other hand, an extensive track record that includes performance data on investments allows the limited partner to review performance by attribution, area, sector, or strategy.

What is not a part of the data room?

The data room should not replace human interactions. Meeting personally with the limited partner is required during the fundraising process. You need the LPs to invest in future funds, so do not lose an opportunity to build a personal relationship.

Should you have a non-disclosure agreement for the data room?

Virtually all data rooms will have a non-disclosure agreement, or NDA, that a limited partner must sign before using the data room. This should be drafted with a lawyer and protect the confidentiality of your materials and information. Be clear on what is covered in the agreement. This documentation ensures that nothing is shared with anyone not authorized to view it. Most LPs will sign, but some institutional LPs may have restrictions around what they are able to sign. You may then need to negotiate the NDA with the limited partner.

CHAPTER 4

Creating A Fundraising Plan — Targeting Limited Partners, Pre-marketing, And A Flexible Mindset

The secret to success is the consistency of purpose.

—Benjamin Disraeli

You have all of the fundraising materials ready to go! I know you are ready to start sending these materials to limited partners. But wait! It makes sense to create a fundraising plan. This plan should be simple and remain flexible. The following advice will guide you to the official fundraising stage, where you share all your materials with targeted limited partners.

Create A List Of Target Limited Partners

Why create a fundraising plan to reach out to LPs?

It is important to take the time upfront to develop a strong fundraising plan. Target limited partners that you know personally or from whom the probability of a warm reception is high. This provides a strong foundation for your fundraising efforts. If you are a single venture capitalist, be disciplined about creating a thorough plan. If there are several partners, sit down together and figure out who will lead the process, how the responsibilities will be divided, what the time commitments of respective partners will be, and how each venture capitalist will engage with the limited partners. Having a plan helps you stay organized and gives you guidance when you start the fundraising process.

One of the most difficult tasks during fundraising is figuring out which of the LPs would be interested in investing in your fund. There is no shortcut here. It will take patience and research as well as confidence in reaching out and building relationships with LPs. Then toss in a bit of luck and circumstance at the end.

Once you have developed a list of LPs with whom to speak, you can use a variety of customer relationship management (CRM) software tools to keep track. Excel, Google sheets, Air Table, or something similar can be used. Just be sure to keep track of who you would like to talk to, who you have talked to, when you talked to them, and any follow-up items.

Make it a part of your process to update this list consistently, ideally after every meeting with a limited partner. Also, be sure to create a cadence for providing updates to those LPs you have already spoken with so they can track your progress. A "no" at the start may turn into a "yes" months later after the LPs have gotten to know the investment team better through personal interactions and informational updates.

Who eventually ends up on your target limited partner list? That depends on who you know, who your friends are, who their friends are, what your fund strategy is, which of the targeted LPs are committing to new funds, as well as other factors. It is important to conduct reference checks on existing and prospective LPs, just as they will conduct checks on you during diligence.

Find out how these LPs have engaged with the venture capitalists they invest in during these checks. Do they meet their capital call commitments in a timely fashion? Can they be valuable, contributing members of an advisory board? Are they actively investing in new funds? Do they expect to work with you in other ways, such as being a co-investor? In Silicon Valley, there is a group of venture capitalists that create WhatsApp groups and other forms of communication to talk about which LPs are investing, into what and with whom. See if you can join one of these groups or get plugged into these conversations and networks.

Why choose a particular limited partner?

A co-founder of a well-established firm best explained the attractive character-istics of LPs. Included in the list are:

- Historical dedication to venture capital

- Ability to be long-term supporters

- Belief in and respect for the venture capital firm's vision and strategy

- Knowledge of venture capital and ability to offer advice

- Strong references from other venture capitalists

Why check the list twice for accreditation?

You have your list ready, but before you start reaching out, be sure that the lim-ited partner is accredited. A venture capitalist is only able to take capital commitments from an accredited investor. In the United States, the Securities and Exchange Commission (SEC) defines what an accredited investor is in Rule 501 of Regulation D. You are responsible for verifying that the LPs investing in your fund are accredited.

It may make sense to check for accreditation through a questionnaire. At the beginning stage, it is an educated guess as to whether the limited partner is ac-credited, but at some point during the process, you may want to request files to verify qualification, such as account information, financial statements, tax re-turns, W-2 forms, or an official letter from a tax or wealth advisor.

The SEC defines accredited investors as follows:

For individuals: An accredited investor must meet one or both of the following criteria:

- Earned income must exceed two hundred thousand (or three hundred thousand with a spouse) in each of the prior two years and expect the same for the current year.

- Have a net worth of more than one million dollars, either alone or with a spouse, excluding the value of the person's primary residence.

For entities: An accredited investor must meet the following criteria:

- Any trust is eligible if it has total assets in excess of five million and was not formed specifically to purchase the subject securities.

- Is an entity in which all of the equity owners are accredited investors.

The rules are in place to protect all investors; however, there is no agency that oversees whether an investor is accredited. It may be in your best interest to take steps to ensure the investors are accredited.

What is the best way to discover LPs?

Leverage your network! The best way to discover engaged and compatible LPs is through venture capitalists who have already raised venture capital funds. But why would another venture capitalist, a potential competitor, introduce you to LPs? Those venture capitalists may believe your strategy complements theirs, making you a value-added member of the venture capital ecosystem, or perhaps the venture capitalist has an oversubscribed fund and is sharing names of LPs with additional dollars they might invest in your fund.

Another way to meet LPs is through other LPs who know and value your strategy. Limited partners have extensive networks, and although LPs do not invest in many new funds each year, they should know which pools of limited partner capital are being actively invested in new funds. A limited partner not currently investing in your fund can still offer references to others. That said, a limited partner not investing in your fund who is willing to make an introduction to another limited partner does not give the best impression. It does not signal the best alignment that an LP is not investing, unless of course the LP is sending a deal that is out of mandate. For example, an LP that only invests in later-stage private equity is passing your fund to another LP who focuses specifically on VC investing.

A venture capitalist can get ahead of the fundraising process, especially with respect to building a network of prospective LPs, by building relationships with venture capitalists and LPs early. Get warm introductions through friends and colleagues who know senior-level venture capitalists and LPs. Attend conferences focused on venture capital fundraising and attend Annual General Meetings (AGM) to increase success. Annual General Meetings are where venture capitalists and LPs gather yearly to discuss the venture capitalist's investments.

What is the most effective way to find LPs?

During the fundraising process, ask everyone who has connections to LPs to facilitate your connection. Also, The Freedom of Information Act (FOIA) ensures access to public information for those researching which LPs are actively investing in venture capital. The FOIA requires public institutions to disclose their investors. Although it is a start, it will not be a comprehensive list.

These disclosures indicate which institutions actively invest in funds similar to yours. By gathering and interpreting this publicly disclosed information, you can assemble a database of which public institutions are actively investing in venture capital and how much they invest per fund.

There are also online databases that have this information, such as Preqin and Pitchbook. These private databases keep a list of active investors and require a subscription.

Ways to get in touch with LPs

- Experienced venture capitalists

- Other relevant LPs

- Alma mater, e.g., career services database

- Conferences

- Annual meetings of other VCs

- Publicly available information (especially through FOIA)

- Private databases

What is the best way to work with placement agents?

Placement agents help you raise your fund and have deep networks to assist you. They can:

- Connect you with individuals and institutions that will invest in your fund

- Add credibility to your fund because placement agents only take on funds they believe have a good chance of being raised

- Collaborate with you to develop marketing materials

- Help you achieve a smooth fundraising process by coaching you on what to say and how to engage with LPs

Placement agents have large networks of LPs. They know the strategies of LPs in their network and are able to get a quick response from them on whether your fund would be interesting to invest in. Many times, they get a subset of those LPs to invest in the fund (or they don't remain in business). If you are a smaller fund or a first-time fund, some placement agents may not be interested in working with you. This is generally true for venture capital funds under $200 million, though there are some placement agents that do spend time in the smaller fund part of the market. Be prepared with your investment strategy before talking to placement agents. Remember, you are selling your investment fund strategies to the placement agent at the same time they will be selling you on their services. They need to pick you as much as you pick them.

A placement agent costs money, and it could be up to three percent of the capital they help raise. There may be additional costs for those LPs that join you in a future fund. This could be expensive for a first-time fund. Also, placement agents may:

- Make your fundraising feel more like a sales process, rather than an exercise in relationship building

- May not fully understand your strategy if you are pitching a model that is truly different from the market.

Another option other than engaging a placement agent is to bring someone in-house that understands your strategy in a clear, concise way and who can manage the outreach to LPs.

Pre-marketing

What is pre-marketing?

Pre-marketing, or the process of interacting with LPs before fully launching the fundraising process, is important. It will strengthen current limited partner relationships, build relationships with prospective LPs, test the value proposition of your fund pitch, and give you a head start on your fundraising process. You may receive many "no's" during the fundraising process for various reasons, so build as many prospective investor relationships as possible in advance of your fundraising launch.

Pre-marketing is a gray area and can refer to any time before launching into the official fundraising process. Because LPs do not like the pressure of a timeline to invest in a fund, meeting with them when you are not fundraising provides a more relaxed environment in which to establish the relationship and gauge the interest in your investment strategy.

Once you officially start fundraising, it is much more difficult to change your strategy and narrative. Changes may lead LPs to believe you launched fundraising prematurely. A thorough pre-marketing period to gather feedback on the fund will assure that you continue to strengthen your value proposition and get better at having conversations with LPs.

Where should the most pre-marketing time be spent and with whom?

There is no recipe to follow when pre-marketing. Think of pre-marketing as more art than science. While pre-marketing primarily refers to meeting with potential LPs, you could also use this time to meet with experienced venture capitalists. Whoever you meet with should have extensive experience in fund formation and raising venture capital funds. That way they can guide you in the right direction with sound advice that is contextually relevant for your specific strategy.

How much time should you spend on pre-marketing?

Pre-marketing has no time frame, so a few weeks or months is probably adequate, depending on how much experience you already have with fundraising. The more diligent and efficient you are in seeking feedback, the quicker the process should be. At some point, you will have enough feedback to understand how your fund strategy resonates with prospective investors and what chance you have of succeeding.

How do you decide which limited partner to meet with first?

Practice your fund pitch on a few LPs who are less likely to invest. Limited partners will have a difficult time figuring out who you are meeting with first; therefore, you do not have a high risk of offering offense by "practicing" with them.

Once you have the pitch perfected, gain some momentum by talking to investors with a higher probability of investing in your fund. Meet with LPs with whom you have strong relationships and try to get them to invest. Revisit verbal commitments to your fund made during earlier conversations. These are sometimes called soft commitments. Using this structure provides you with additional confidence to move forward.

Try to build strong relationships with a handful of trustworthy LPs. Pitch the fundraising process early on in the relationship. As trusted confidants, they will work through fund ideas and pitches with you before you pitch to the general market. I've worked with a number of venture capitalist funds in this capacity and have seen first-hand fundraising materials that offer advice on both pitch and strategy. It is best to reach out for feedback in the pre-marketing phase before starting the official fundraising process.

A mirror can also work. I'm not talking about Snow White's Magic Mirror, but rather a mirror that delivers an honest appraisal of how prepared you are. Record yourself on video and watch the playback. Critique yourself and ask an objective friend to evaluate the presentation. The more confidence you have in your delivery, the better.

How do venture capitalists ultimately choose the right LPs?

Once venture capitalists begin engaging with LPs, they will realize they have gone down a rabbit hole. A wide variety of LPs invest in venture capital, though in all likelihood, only a handful will be a fit for your fund. Learn which of these LPs from the myriad of investors on your list will be most likely to commit. This is called a process of discovery. You can simply ask LPs whether your fund is a fit for their investment strategy. A quick "no" saves time. Move forward and re-prioritize with whom you should engage.

Many LPs may want more time to research you and your fund to see if it is a fit. Not getting a clear answer can be frustrating, but it is important to remember that LPs are working on multiple investments and going through their own process of prioritization. Concentrate on LPs who are excited about your fund. If progress or communication slows down, be direct but polite, and ask if they plan to invest in the fund. This saves time and may preserve the relationship for the next fund.

Has the limited partner invested in venture capital before?

Investing in venture capital is different from investing in other asset classes, such as public equities. Venture capital investments are higher risk. The funds invested are "locked up" for a longer period of time than in most other asset classes. Limited partners with little venture capital experience may have difficulty adjusting to the aspect of longer duration. Ask about LPs' portfolios and recent fund investments. Know if they have invested in funds similar to yours and when. This can allay some of your concerns over whether they are relevant investors for your current fund or just seeking market intelligence.

What is the motivation of the limited partner for fund investing?

There are many reasons LPs invest in funds. These include getting exposure to venture capital investments while reducing company-specific risk, looking for co-investments, or getting insight into a strategy or industry. Knowing the motivation for each limited partner before he/she invests in your fund can help you better manage the limited partner. For example, if you are a healthcare fund and a pharmaceutical company invests in your fund, perhaps this is a strategic investment for the pharmaceutical company. Knowing this beforehand can improve the relationship.

Is what you do important to the limited partner strategically?

The venture capitalist should have a sense of whether he/she is important to the limited partner. Figure out how big the limited partner is before moving forward. If the firm is a trillion-dollar asset manager that invests a billion dollars into venture capital, then venture capital may or may not be a priority for this type of firm. If you are a venture capital fund and speaking with a fund-of-funds that only invests in venture capital funds, you can be sure that they will be knowledgeable. Know why you are important to the limited partner and how you fit into their strategy long-term. Do not put yourself in a situation where every time you go out to raise a fund, you have to bring on new LPs. The best practice is to think about limited partner relationships on a ten-year horizon and to keep LPs for several funds.

What should the venture capitalist think about before taking capital?

You should have a good understanding of how liquid, competent, and honorable your limited partner is. For example, you should understand the processes for how they meet capital calls (that is, pay you when you need to be paid so you can make investments into companies). While not common, sometimes LPs do not understand the obligation of capital calls or do not have proper processes in place to pay capital calls when called. There could be a variety of reasons for this happening. Limited partners without capital dedicated to venture fund strategy sometimes stop paying capital calls before the fund is over because they "feel like it" or because they lost liquidity for some other reason. Beware that this may occur at even the best institutions during downturns in the economy.

Do the values of the limited partner align with your values?

This point is critical to having a smooth long-term relationship. Limited partners and venture capitalists are aligned because both parties want to make money through investing. Making money should be an ethical practice, so make sure all the LPs you work with are ethical. Does the limited partner care about how you make money? Does the limited partner actually care about the people, lives, jobs, and global impact of the investment? If your values do not fit the LPs' values, then look to the next partnership.

Maintaining A Flexible Mindset

How to maintain flexibility?

Maintain a flexible mindset during the fundraising process. Although you will have an initial plan of who to meet, every plan is guaranteed to change. After speaking with a co-founder of a top international venture capital fund, I learned that he had more than four-hundred-and-fifty limited partner conversations with only a five percent success rate in getting them to invest in the fund, not unusual for a success rate. It illustrates that being organized and staying streamlined helps you meet with the large number of LPs needed to close your fund.

Circumstances can change. Listen carefully to feedback and adjust the plan if needed. Decide which LPs are interested enough in your fund that they will invest. Know which LPs are active in the market and committing to new funds. Get a number of introductions to new LPs who are qualified and have a high likelihood of being potential investors in your fund.

Always be fundraising. Whether you are in the market with a fund or if creating a venture fund is just a distant thought, carry yourself as if you are planning to kick off a formal fundraising process.

Unless you are a known entity in the venture capital world, it will be difficult to raise capital from institutional investors, including endowments, foundations, and pension funds. You will probably have to wait through a fund cycle or two before they will invest into your fund. Often the people running institutional limited partner pools of capital know the established venture capital funds well and only invest with known venture capital investors who have existing track records and who are leaving established firms to start new ones.

Many times, these LPs will get a call from another venture capitalist who has demonstrated returns for the Limited Partners in the past, telling the Limited Partners that they should invest in a first-time fund. A strong recommendation from a venture capitalist is more meaningful than all the feedback you could get from CEOs.

What are some regulatory issues to talk to your lawyer about?

Talk time with your lawyer is requisite before moving on with the process. Ensure that this is a fund formation lawyer, preferably one who has worked with other venture capital funds, to gain the professional advice and guidance you'll need. If you ask a well-known venture capital firm or a respected third-party service provider for recommendations, they will be able to list several lawyers relevant for your strategy. Limited partners do not like complex documents and terms. A lawyer will help structure your fund in a simple and straightforward way.

There are certain laws you must be familiar with before advancing to a higher level in the process. Learn them before taking on investors in the fund. For example, a United States law called the Investment Advisers Act, also known as the Investment Advisers Act of 1940, is a federal law created to monitor and regulate the activities of investment advisers. This law is administered by the United States Securities and Exchange Commission (SEC) and governs a number of fund specific regulations.

PHASE 2:
FUNDRAISING

CHAPTER 5

Reaching Out To And Interacting With Limited Partners

Flaming enthusiasm, backed by horse sense and persistence,
is the quality that most frequently makes for success.

—Dale Carnegie

Pre-marketing Is Over: Let The FUN-draising Begin

How do you begin the fun?

For first-time fundraisers, reaching out to limited partners may be daunting. There are many questions to be answered. Who are LPs? Where do I find them? What's the best way to get in touch with LPs? What do I say to LPs? How do I interact with LPs to optimize my chances of success? Should I take what LPs say at face value, or is there a secret code I should understand to decide whether they are actually interested?

These questions are all important. Be smart about engaging with LPs. Do your research upfront. Be efficient when meeting with LPs and be respectful of their time and yours. Be flexible and self-aware enough to know who will actually give you money this time around versus who is just entertaining you. Remember, your time is valuable, and you want to raise the capital as quickly as possible so you can get back to finding and investing in great companies.

Make sure the LPs are interested in your fund strategy. For example, if you are a seed-stage venture capital fund investing in seed companies, and your prospective limited partner only invests in late-stage public market stocks, this is obviously not a good fit. Seek perfect alignment between the venture capital fund and the limited partner's investment strategies.

The people or institutions that could potentially invest in you and your fund idea appreciate determination. Think of fundraising as part of a numbers game. Limited partners are inherently curious and will probably attend a meeting just to understand where you fit in the venture capital universe. They will do this even if there is a low probability that they will invest. Nevertheless, you should make time for these meetings. These meetings will still help you gain confidence, might garner introductions to other LPs, and will keep LPs updated on your progress.

It might be a long time before the fund is raised, so have a method of tracking all your communications with LPs. If you have a well-run process that ultimately persuades just a few more LPs to invest, that can be a successful fundraiser.

There will be many other venture capitalists fundraising at the same time as you and they, too, are trying to impress. Limited partners look at hundreds of venture capital funds each year, but they may also invest across other strategies, such as private equity funds and hedge funds. Show LPs that your experience aligns with what you are trying to achieve with your investment strategy. Persuade the limited partner that you are the right fiduciary for their capital. Great communication skills, sales skills, patience, and flexibility are your friends.

Contacting And Interacting With Limited Partners

Who are LPs?

Limited partners are individuals with their own ideas and judgements as investors. They can make or break your fund opportunity by investing—or not. They become your client if they invest. Operating within the confines of what LPs expect from the venture capitalist is a path to success.

Where do you find LPs?

Use your network. If you are raising a fund, you probably have connections to LPs already. If you already know some LPs, reach out directly to them. Based on the list of LPs you have already created, figure out if people you know have established relationships with these LPs and ask them for warm introductions. LinkedIn is a good tool for connecting to LPs.

In addition to LinkedIn, there are other databases where you can find lists of LPs, such as Preqin and Pitchbook. Attending conferences is another way to meet or hear about LPs who are aligned with your strategies. Look for conferences that are dedicated to LPs, such as those put on by the Institutional Limited Partner Association (ILPA). There are other conferences with a disproportionate number of LPs attending, including conferences focused only on family offices. A conference is an opportunity to establish credibility with the limited partner and to give him/her a sense that you are networking to make your fundraising process a success.

What's the best way to get in touch with a limited partner?

Get an introduction to a limited partner from a close mutual acquaintance. Keep the initial exchange short and to the point. The limited partner probably will already know if your fund is a fit even before you send the initial email. Consider other forms of communication, as well. Twitter or other social media platforms used by the limited partner for professional exchanges may be used, but avoid platforms he/she uses solely for personal matters. Attend conferences where VCs and LPs exchange market intelligence. Conferences can be hit or miss events, but it is worth the effort to go.

Where should you dedicate the most time when engaging with LPs?

Seek out those LPs where there is a high probability of getting a commitment.

What should you expect when dealing with LPs?

Be prepared to meet with LPs over an extended period of time and expect the decision-making timeline to take months and sometimes even years. Each fundraising process with each limited partner will be different. Experienced investors in high demand may have only one meeting with the limited partner. It is more likely, however—especially if you are new to fundraising and raising your first fund—that there will be several meetings.

How should you interact with a limited partner over the course of a typical fundraising process?

Meetings differ but all should be regarded as important. A sample schedule of meetings for a simple fundraising process could look like this:

1. You have an initial meeting with the limited partner to walk through your pitch deck.

2. A follow-up meeting is held a few weeks later to dive deeper on a particular subject in your pitch deck.

3. A third meeting introduces the limited partner to other instrumental members of your team, such as other investment partners or data scientists helping you execute your strategy.

4. As part of operational due diligence, you have a meeting call with the limited partner to answer questions about the operations of your fund.

If you have a CFO or similar person at the firm, then he/she may be the appropriate person to handle the ODD questions.

5. Negotiate terms of legal due diligence over the course of several meetings and calls involving your lawyers.

The above is just an example of possible interactions with the limited partner during a fundraising process. The actual interactions might differ from those described here, but the general outline holds true. These meetings should begin to build trust between you, your team, and the limited partner. Once that trust is established, share the investment strategy, and explain why investing in your fund is an attractive opportunity that will make the LPs money. Who attends these meetings is important. Decision makers and influencers should be at the table.

Initial Meeting

When should the initial meeting take place?

Meet with LPs that you know well as soon as possible and discuss your strategy. For those you do not know yet, make sure you have a solid strategy and story before taking a meeting. You could come across as unprofessional if you are not sufficiently prepared. Have a document ready that supports your strategy, such as a pitch deck that outlines your investment strategy and the details of the fund. Then set up an initial meeting.

When it is clear that you are moving forward with the fundraising process, other documents will be needed, but these can be developed during ensuing discussions with the LPs.

How should you set up the initial meeting?

Limited partners who invest in venture capital are distributed globally. You could spend a lot of time traveling to in-person visits. One way to overcome this geographical challenge is to qualify prospective LPs through emails or phone calls. If the limited partner seems interested, schedule a meeting. The meeting might take place in the limited partner's office, or you could invite him/her to meet when they are in your area. As a venture capitalist, have a sense of your time schedule so you can decide whether it is practical to visit the limited partner. If the limited partner always insists you make the visit, it could mean the limited partner is overstretched.

Who should be there for the initial meeting?

The decision-makers should attend the initial meeting. For venture capitalists, this means the partners responsible for investing capital. For LPs, this means individuals responsible for investing into venture capital funds. Having the right people in the room is important when beginning a relationship with a new limited partner. A full team in attendance allows the LPs to assess team dynamics, but this does not pertain to single venture capitalists.

The same rule applies for LPs: the decision-makers should be in the room. A decision-maker is the partner who ultimately makes the decision on whether to bring your fund opportunity forward to be discussed as a potential investment.

Venture capitalists should be aware that non-partners at larger limited partner institutions may also play a role in sourcing new fund investment opportunities. Though not partners, they can influence decisions. Some may already have investment obligations to existing venture capitalists, or they may be eager to find the next great investment opportunity. They should not be overlooked as they may become the heavy lifters in the process by reviewing the fund quantitatively, by making reference calls, or by writing the investment memo for the investment committee. They are investors who want to partner with great people and to find great investments. Meeting with them can set the tone for success.

How should you prepare for the initial meeting?

Spend time on a well-thought-out pitch deck before the initial meeting and be sure you have answered questions about why you are different. Know your competitive advantage as an investor and your investment thesis. Be well prepared for the questions that the LPs will ask.

Here are some questions that could be asked by LPs in an initial meeting:

1. Can you tell us about your team?

2. Do you expect to add to the team over the course of this fund?

3. Why are you raising a venture capital fund?

4. What makes you different from the other venture capital funds?

5. What is your investment strategy?

6. What stage companies will you invest in?

7. What are your ownership targets?

8. How much capital will you reserve for follow-on investments?

9. Will you lead investments, or will you co-invest alongside other lead investors?

10. How many investments do you expect to have in your fund portfolio?

11. What companies have you invested in previously?

12. Are there any companies you are actively in discussions with that may end up in the portfolio?

This is not a complete list by any means. It simply illustrates the types of questions that will be asked by LPs. Be prepared to answer these questions in your pitch deck and at the meeting.

How do LPs prepare to meet with you?

Limited partners should have read all of the materials shared with them before the initial meeting. Based on the materials, good LPs will also prepare insightful questions in advance. Though some LPs send an agenda with the main topics and questions they would like to cover during the initial meeting, it is recommended that the venture capitalist send it.

Good LPs leverage their network in advance of the meeting by asking for references. This reference phase could happen even before a meeting is set up to help the limited partner determine if it is necessary to meet. A limited partner decides whether to take a first meeting by listening to other LPs who have already met with the venture capitalist. He/she will also gather feedback from other venture capitalists or founders who have worked with the fund raiser in the past. Then a judgement call is made on whether a meeting is worthwhile.

What do you want out of the initial meeting?

At the initial meeting, you should have explained who you are and what your fund will do. You should emerge from the meeting with an understanding of what the limited partner wants to invest in. In some cases, the limited partner will be transparent and disclose during the initial meeting whether the fund is a fit and whether the process will continue. But, if he/she does not, ask the limited partner whether it makes sense to continue the conversation because the fundraising process will probably take more time than you planned. Therefore, get to the "yes" or "no" as soon as possible.

What does the limited partner want out of the initial meeting?

The limited partner meets with dozens or even hundreds of venture capitalists each year. These meetings may be over the phone or in-person. He/she will not end up investing in every single fund for which a meeting is planned. In this first meeting, the limited partner wants to assess whether the fund is a fit for the LP's portfolio.

What are the expectations of the limited partner when meeting?

An initial meeting is a strong start because the limited partner has already seen something in the fund strategy that is attractive. The limited partner will use the initial meeting to determine whether it makes sense to have a follow-up meeting and potentially kick off a due diligence process. The limited partner wants to answer as many outstanding questions as possible. The more comfortable the limited partner is with the investment opportunity, the better.

Limited partners sit in a privileged position as the capital allocators. Sometimes, they will meet with no intention of investing in your fund just to gather information about you, your fund, your prior fund, or the market in which you're investing. This can be a tricky piece of the fundraising process because if LPs agree to meet with you, they expect transparency about your strategies. Choose to meet with LPs who have available capita, an investment strategy for investing in the fund, and a recent history of investing in funds similar to yours. You must convince the limited partner you will execute well on your strategy and make money.

What questions will LPs ask when the VC leaves the room after the initial meeting?

Limited partners will determine whether any follow-ups are necessary with the venture capitalist by asking a number of questions, including:

- How did the meeting go?
- Did the limited partner and the venture capitalist get along i.e., could you work as a partner with this team for the next 10-25 years?
- What new information was presented, and did it contribute to making a better decision about whether to invest in the venture capitalist?
- Is the limited partner excited about the performance, team, strategy, portfolio, construction, and market?
- Does the limited partner want to set up a follow-up meeting?

- Are there restrictions that could prevent the limited partner from investing that came up during the meeting?
- Were there any yellow or red flags raised during the meeting? Were there moments that caused the limited partner to doubt whether the venture capitalist can execute the strategy?
- If there are yellow flags, are there discrete follow-up items that the limited partner should research?
- If there were red flags, can they be resolved?

When will LPs respond to VCs?

Limited partners should respond to venture capitalists as soon as they have discussed the investment opportunity and have decided whether they want to continue the process. Venture capitalists involved in a fundraising process are probably talking to large numbers of LPs and to have a clear answer helps them to hone their investment process.

What are the signs that it has been a good meeting?

This is a tricky question. Even if a meeting goes well, the limited partner still may not invest in your fund. The best practice is to know how the limited partner would like to proceed and whether the venture capitalist can provide ongoing updates to track all progress. Listen to how the limited partner wants to engage going forward and use this feedback as a guideline for future interactions. Remember that "no may just mean no" for now. It can change to "yes" as the fund opportunity progresses and as the venture capitalist lines up other LPs and builds the team.

How do you ask the limited partner for feedback so you don't waste a lot of time?

Feedback is a way to improve the fund and the firm. When a limited partner passes on a current fund opportunity, find out why. Sometimes the limited partner just wants to wait until the fund has been around longer so he/she can see how the team works together, what types of companies are being invested in, and other factors that can only be assessed over a longer period of time. For example, a pause in working with an investment partner or an unsolvable characteristic of the fund in the near-term could cause concern for a limited partner. Work to mitigate any risk for the limited partner and re-engage after raising the current fund and in advance of the next fund.

What does the limited partner expect from the venture capitalist as a follow-up?

During the initial meeting, the LPs and venture capitalists discuss the next steps. This keeps the fundraising process moving forward. Based on this conversation, the venture capitalist should have an idea of what the limited partner expects as follow up. Part of that follow up could be sending additional materials on questions that came up during the diligence meeting. If the limited partner passed on the fund during the meeting but asked to be included in future updates, keep the limited partner informed. It is the venture capitalist's responsibility to know what the limited partner expects and to follow through on those expectations. This will impress the limited partner.

What materials will LPs typically ask for after the meeting?

What LPs ask for after the initial meeting depends on what has already been shared. If it was a good meeting, the limited partner will ask for more fundraising materials, including access to the data room. The data room should hold all the fundraising documents required for the limited partner to make a decision. Ideally, the venture capitalist provides access to the data room as quickly as possible, perhaps even the same day that it is requested.

There are some fundraising materials that may not be disclosed early on, such as the reference list of people who have worked with the venture capitalist in the past. Limited partners may ask for this list with the intention of calling those references.

If specific questions were raised during the meeting, such as questions about the market, then the limited partner may ask for supporting materials to become comfortable with these issues.

How much will LPs ask for additionally?

Limited partners ask for the fundraising materials necessary for them to make an investment decision. The documents covered in this book are adequate to address most of the questions and concerns LPs will want answered during the due diligence process. However, because each limited partner has his/her own concerns, additional information may be needed.

For each request, determine how much preparation time will be required. If asked for some ad hoc diligence not required by other LPs, ask other venture capitalists if it is common. Have the confidence to determine whether a request is too demanding given the time constraints during a fundraising process. Talk openly with LPs about ways to simplify the request so it does not infringe on other priorities.

Are there other LPs who have already committed?

The network of LPs tends to be insular. Most know each other and talk to each other. After an initial meeting, LPs will try to determine which other LPs are investing. Sometimes this will be asked directly during the meeting. It is the right of the venture capitalist to answer selectively.

If investments of other LPs are disclosed, expect the limited partner to talk to those LPs. This can be good because those committed to the fund can persuade other LPs to do the same.

Follow-up Meeting

Why might there be a follow-up meeting?

A follow-up meeting is a good sign that the limited partner is interested in the fund. The venture capitalist and limited partner are developing a relationship, and this requires face-to-face meetings. During a follow-up meeting, the limited partner is trying to answer more specific questions about the fund. The limited partner is also trying to get a good sense of the venture capitalist and wants to continue building a foundation of trust with him/her.

Who should attend the follow up meeting?

The attendees will be largely the same as those at the initial meeting. Many times, the limited partner will have his/her own internal "sales process" to convince other members of his investment team to commit to the venture capitalist. This may mean that more people will be in follow-up meetings, including more members of the Investment Committee.

Where is the best place for a follow-up meeting?

The best place for a follow-up meeting can be anywhere. I would encourage you to have the limited partner come to your office if possible. Seeing your office is a way for the limited partner to get a sense of how you work. It is an opportunity to shed some light on your day-to-day experience. If you do not have an office that can accommodate a meeting, then meet at the limited partner's office or a mutually convenient place.

How should you prepare for the follow-up meeting?

This is when the "two ears, one mouth" mantra you were taught as a kid comes into play. Listen carefully to the limited partner's questions and be prepared to answer them. Also, circulate an agenda before the meeting so you stay focused during the allotted time.

What do you want out of the follow-up meeting?

As with the initial meeting, you want to see continued progress in the second meeting. Be sure you have followed up on all outstanding questions from the initial meeting. Limited partners like to invest in individuals who are competent and able to follow through on their plans.

What should you think about as you approach a follow-up meeting?

Take your cue from what the limited partner would like to discuss. The limited partner is trying to become comfortable with making an investment in the fund throughout the diligence process. The venture capitalist is trying to make the limited partner comfortable with any concerns or questions about the investment. Avoid disclosing too much information at once. Be efficient with the fundraising information process and address any questions about risks raised by the limited partner.

The follow-up meeting, or any meeting after the one where you go through your high-level pitch, should be focused on the concerns of the limited partner. Any follow-up meetings should be held as soon as possible after the initial meeting. This is especially important if you would like the limited partner involved in your fund. Determine whether the limited partner structurally requires a longer diligence process. For example, endowments may only meet with the Board of Directors once a quarter to finalize investment decisions. You may have to wait at least three months to get to a final decision.

Processing Feedback

What are the ways in which LPs might respond to you and to your fund?

Remember that each limited partner will have a response unique to that limited partner. Your goal should be to get a clear and direct response from the limited partner as soon as possible. The truth is—some LPs go silent after a period of time. This could mean they are actively working through diligence or that they have parallel fundraising processes that make it difficult to concentrate on your fund. Your responsibility is to figure out the reason. Be transparent and use a Customer Relationship Management (CRM) tool or e-mail integration to track touch points with the limited partner.

How many follow up meetings will there be in total?

There is no minimum or maximum number of meetings during the diligence process with a limited partner. If you already know the limited partner well, then at least one in-person meeting is recommended, ideally at the venture capitalist's office. This is referred to as an "onsite meeting." This meeting could answer all the questions needed to convince the limited partner to invest in your fund.

How do you know if it is worth continuing the conversation with a limited partner?

You will know whether to continue the conversation with a limited partner after the initial meeting, especially if the limited partner gives transparent and direct feedback. Remember, you are trying to reduce the amount of time you spend with LPs who are not going to invest in your fund. Therefore, try to get a clear answer as soon as possible.

CHAPTER 6

Due Diligence

Diligence is the mother of good luck.

—Benjamin Franklin

Due Diligence

Introduction to due diligence

The due diligence process is like most steps in the fundraising process: what seems confusing and daunting at first is actually quite simple. Thinking about broad concepts such as due diligence, operational due diligence, and legal due diligence can be confusing, as can understanding how they relate to the limited partners' approach to evaluating your fund. How do you, the venture capitalist, make sense of these various parts of fund evaluation? And what parts are relevant to you to help you become more successful in raising your fund?

By now, you are well on your way to raising your venture capital fund; you have reached out to relevant LPs and are engaging with them. Perhaps you have some commitments already from non-institutional friends and family investors. The institutional LPs may even be digging into the details of your fund and asking more questions or planning follow-up meetings with you.

Now what? How do you continue this positive momentum to get limited partners to invest in your fund? Being knowledgeable about the parts of the process and knowing what Limited Partners are thinking is a start to managing an efficient and thorough due diligence process.

You should know what the limited partners are doing during each phase, how they are doing it, and why they are doing it. This can be helpful for you as you prepare presentations. Limited partners want to invest in funds that have reduced risk, that have a good chance of returning multiples of invested capital, and that have positive views as being good fiduciaries of their capital. Doing the work to set up your fund legally and preparing robust fundraising materials is a good start. Combine this with your background, track record, and experience, and you have just become an attractive fund investment opportunity.

What is due diligence?

Due diligence is the process through which a limited partner determines whether to invest in a venture capital fund. This process involves research conducted by the limited partners over a period of time to gauge the risks of an investment opportunity. Limited partners may take anywhere from a few weeks to several years to get to know a venture capitalist before investing. I once took over a due diligence process that was seven years in the making. The investment team had met consistently with the management team of the fund for seven years, tracking the growth of the organization and its performance. Year seven turned out to be lucky for this fund manager, and we finally committed to the fund after recognizing the firm's market dominance. Don't be discouraged; this is an outlier example of how long it took to gain the confidence to invest in the opportunity. The lesson here is patience can be a virtue in the due diligence process.

The goal of due diligence is to get a good understanding of the investment risks. Once these risks are assessed, if the limited partners still have confidence of a high return, they will make the investment. If the limited partners have low confidence or remain uncertain about the potential return, they will probably not invest. Your goal should be to push them over this hurdle by giving them more clarity and data.

Two perspectives of due diligence

Limited partner's perspective: From the limited partner's perspective, the goal of due diligence should assess the risks of the venture capitalist fund and allow him/her to gain confidence in the investment opportunity. There are various types of risks. There can be risks related to the team, to the fund strategy, or to the market. During due diligence, limited partners decide if the benefits outweigh the risks.

Venture capitalist's perspective: From the venture capitalist's perspective, the goal of due diligence process should be about mitigating risks. After reading this chapter, you should have an understanding of the risks that Limited Partners will consider. Limited partners will look at a venture capitalist fund from many different perspectives, so the venture capitalist should review risks associated with his/her team, strategy, and market opportunity. Responses to potential weaknesses or gaps in the proposal should be prepared. Ask close colleagues for constructive criticism if you have difficulty identifying risks. For example, the venture capitalist could actually point out potential risks and show why these risks are under control.

Limited partners are charged with gathering information and data about the venture capitalist. The venture capitalist discloses to the limited partner the vast majority of this information in the shared fundraising materials. The more thorough the materials, the more information the LPs will have to make an investment case to their organizations on your behalf. This may result in a commitment to your fund.

These fundraising materials can include a pitch deck, due diligence questionnaire (DDQ), private placement memorandum (PPM), Limited Partnership Agreement (LPA), and a number of other documents whose disclosure may be important. The limited partner uses these fundraising materials, in addition to other research such as reference calls, to make a decision on whether to invest.

The main fundraising materials:

Pitch deck: a presentation developed by the venture capitalist to describe the venture capital fund, usually between 10-30 slides

Due diligence questionnaire (DDQ): a document put together by the venture capitalist to address questions and concerns that arise from the due diligence process

Private placement memorandum (PPM): a (many times lengthy) document put together by the venture capitalist that includes information on fund strategy, the market opportunity, and the terms of the investment

Limited partnership agreement (LPA): a legal document developed by the venture capitalist (alongside a law firm) defining the terms of the venture capital fund

---

A venture capitalist will continue to raise capital and regularly pitch ideas to the Limited Partners to enhance the possibility of investment. It is advisable that the venture capitalist provide the limited partners with quality information and data during this process. This chapter will help you understand the various fundraising materials used by a venture capitalist and their individual strengths.

What is an example of a due diligence process?

A due diligence process can include meetings between the venture capitalist and the limited partners, review of fundraising materials, assessment of the operations of the venture capitalist's firm, and references from companies with which a venture capitalist has previously invested. The way different Limited Partners move through the due diligence process can depend on a variety of factors, including schedule, mandate, or familiarity with the team or strategy.

The following is an example of a due diligence process:

- Limited partners are introduced to a venture capitalist fund investment opportunity via a trusted contact—perhaps through a CEO who knows the VC directly after working together on committed investments in the CEO's company.

- The VC follows up on this introduction by sending a short email explaining the fund strategy and submitting a pitch deck for the LPs to review.

- The LPs review the pitch deck and decide if the venture capitalist is right for their investment strategy.

- The LPs request an initial call with the VC. (Sometimes this initial meeting may be in-person if convenient for both parties.)

- If, after the initial call, the LPs and the VC realize that there is an alignment of their strategies, an in-person meeting is scheduled to go deeper and begin building a relationship. Few (if any) LPs commit to a VC fund without first meeting with the investment team in person.

- If the in-person meeting goes well, then the LPs may ask for a data room and start to collect references on the VC to get a better sense of past performance and credibility. Many times, the LPs will start seeking references from within their own network. These could be from friends and colleagues that are in common with the VC. The LPs may then ask for a formal reference list, which is provided by the VC.

- The VC shares the data room with the LPs and provides other disclosures to help the LPs understand the investment opportunity.

- The LPs review the data room and have an internal discussion with more members of the LPs' team.

- The LPs may continue to make reference calls to CEOs, venture capitalists, and other individuals who have worked with the VC in the past.

- At this point, it is clear that the LPs are engaged in the due diligence process because they are spending money and time on evaluating the fund. The LPs indicate their interest in the fund, and it goes before the LPs' investment committees to decide whether to invest or not. There may be additional approvals for institutional LPs, such as Board approval as an oversight in addition to the LP investment committee.

- The LPs review the operations of the firm (operational due diligence) and the Limited Partnership Agreement (legal due diligence), and they provide comments to the venture capitalist for term changes (legal due diligence).

- The VC assesses, negotiates, and revises the LPA for the LPs after collecting comments from all of them and returns an updated copy.

- The VC has indicated a target close date, and the LPs submit subscription agreements to the VC after having reviewed them with a lawyer.

- The VC collects subscription agreements from multiple Limited Partners and closes on the fund in coordination with their law firm.

This is a simplified process, but it gives an idea of the back and forth, as well as the various steps in any due diligence process. Even in the rare case where your reputation precedes you and the limited partner says yes at the first meeting, you will still have other parts in the investment process to complete.

What's the difference between due diligence, operational due diligence, and legal due diligence?

Due Diligence: This term is used in two ways. It refers to everything in the overall process of a limited partner assessing an investment opportunity. Due diligence, operational due diligence, and legal due diligence all fall in this category. There are distinct parts to the diligence process, however, and due diligence can also refer to assessing the investment opportunity by investment team performance. Specifically, this refers to evaluating the track record and making reference calls to understand how venture capitalists' teams have been helpful to companies.

Operational Due Diligence: The process by which the LPs assess the risks of the firm's operations. For example, how does a VC manage its valuation or audit process? At larger LPs, there are separate teams that cover this part of the diligence.

Legal Due Diligence: The process of reviewing the Limited Partnership Agreement (LPA), which can include a comprehensive review of the fund terms. It is also when the LP and the VC negotiate other terms and arrangements outside of the LPA, usually through additional legal documents called side letters.

Why will developing a Private Placement Memorandum (PPM) help LPs with due diligence?

A Private Placement Memorandum, also referred to as an offering memorandum, is a legal document sent to prospective investors. It provides information on the prospective fund investment.

The PPM is a business plan. While the PPM can organize information in a comprehensive way for prospective LPs, it is sometimes viewed as unnecessary by both LPs and VCs. Despite all the time and effort that goes into preparing a PPM, many LPs do not read it completely. Still, it can serve as a useful reference document; an example is when the LP is writing an investment memo for an investment committee. It gives LPs a comprehensive view of the fund strategy, the market opportunity, and the terms of the investment.

What are the main sections in a PPM?

- Introduction

- Management Team

- Investment Strategy

- Investment Objective

- Offering Terms

- Risk Factors

- Tax Implications

What do LPs look for during due diligence?

In addition to investment performance, the team, and the strategy, LPs will consider market opportunity, portfolio construction, and the economics of the fund.

What are some common questions that LPs ask about performance?

- What is the VC's past investment performance (also referred to as attribution or track record)?

- How consistent has his/her performance been over time?

- Has the VC invested in multiple great companies, or is he/she a "one hit wonder"?

- What are the underlying companies in the VC's portfolio, and are the companies generating revenues and making accelerated progress?

- Has the VC invested in companies that have become the leading companies in their industries?

- What was the VC's role in investing in the company; for example, discovering the company, building relationships with the CEO to get investment allocation, or sitting on the Board of Directors?

How do LPs look at investment performance, attribution, and track record?

For investment performance, the LPs look at whether you actually sourced and invested in the company. What is your track record in finding and investing in great companies? If a venture capitalist has a track record of investing in ten companies, the LPs will look at each of those companies to determine whether they are strong investments, what their current fair market value is, and the operating metrics of those companies. In addition to growth in portfolio companies, LPs will also look at whether the VC sold its companies or had any that went public. In particular, institutional LPs want VCs that have invested in other companies and helped build substantial companies that generated significant value. Expect LPs to review your entire portfolio of past investments. Be ready to disclose this list and talk knowledgably about all of your portfolio companies.

Definition of track record

The portfolio of companies that a VC has invested in is called the track record. For the LP who wants to invest in a fund, the track record shows that a VC has been able to identify valuable investment opportunities. A track record is acquired by finding and investing in companies over a period of time and managing those companies to success.

What are underwriting criteria for companies? A good LP knows markets and companies well. A good LP is able to assess companies in a fund or portfolio and determine how likely they are to succeed. If the companies are valuable, the LPs will be more interested in investing, expecting that the VC will continue to find and invest in similarly attractive companies.

Most institutional LPs look for an investment performance that has two characteristics.

The first characteristic is an attractive return, which in venture capital is anything more than three times the return on the cost of the total investments. For example, if one hundred million dollars was invested in the past, and that cost basis is now held at three hundred million dollars in value, then it represents a good investment performance.

The second characteristic is "realized returns." Having three hundred million dollars looks great, but if that value is not converted to cash and distributed to the limited partner, then the value is less attractive. Has the VC in the past returned money to his/her LPs? The LPs will have greater confidence in backing a VC that has returned capital to LPs in the past.

How do LPs assess the investment team?

The team is another important factor that LPs think about when considering an investment opportunity. Some common questions LPs ask are the following:

- Who are the VCs?

- Where do the VCs come from, meaning, were they formerly company founders, operators, investors, or something else?

- How complementary are the team members in terms of perspectives and skill sets?

- If they were formerly founders or operators, at which companies and what impact did they have?

- If they were formerly investors, at which VC or investment firms did they work? What experience do they have, especially relating to the current fund strategy? What role did they play in the investment process at their prior firms?

- What is their network, especially as it relates to sourcing new investments?

- How good is the VC's reputation among founders, other VCs, and LPs?

- Why is this VC team the best team for the fund strategy?

- How will this VC differentiate itself from other VC teams with similar strategies?

- How long have the VCs been investing?

- What is their investment performance, by partner and as a team?

- Are they long-term thinkers and do they plan to remain VCs?

How do LPs evaluate your investment strategy?

Strategy can determine whether the LP will take a look at an investment opportunity. When looking at a seed stage-focused investor, some LPs may choose not to meet because such funds are too high risk and outside the scope of their own investment strategy. For example, when blockchain and crypto funds began to emerge, LPs viewed the unproven business opportunity as too high risk, and therefore many avoided investing into this type of VC fund. It is important to determine the LPs' focus for their fund strategy early on. Make sure your fund strategies match theirs before spending too much time on pitching to them.

How do LPs evaluate the market opportunity?

LPs may decide whether the fund fits their investment strategy based on factors such as market opportunity. For instance, if a specialized fund focuses only on food technology, LPs with different strategies not focused on food technology may not want to meet. It is important to know this early in the process. It is probable that institutional LPs focused on venture capital are set in their viewpoints and strategies. If they do not like something before the meeting, they probably will not like it after the meeting.

Best practice provides LPs with materials that translate quickly to knowledge about the market opportunity. With enough supporting information and internal research, the LPs may change their minds, especially if you are consistent, clear, and persuasive in teaching them about the market opportunity. Given time is a constraint, the best practice is to focus on LPs who already show an interest in your strategy and market.

LPs may also make decisions based on geography. For example, some LPs will not invest in venture capital in Europe. These LPs will not take a first meeting if you are based in Europe and investing in Europe.

The key point is many LPs have set strategies. It is better to find LPs with strategies that align with yours.

What do LPs think about portfolio construction and what is the implication for making investment returns on your invested capital?

Portfolio construction refers to how the VC finances investments in the portfolio. In public markets, there are public disclosures that allow investors to know what they are buying. In venture capital, the LPs do not know what they are buying into at the portfolio level. Therefore, the LP has to learn how the portfolio will be assembled by the VC during the life of the portfolio.

The LP asks several questions to understand how the money will be invested. For example, how many companies will you invest in, at what stage, and how will you finance these companies over time? Will you invest all the capital in round one with the companies, or will you reserve capital to invest in those same companies in follow-up rounds? For institutional LPs, the heart of portfolio construction is the belief that high ownership in companies results in better performance, or you have access to a high number of the greatest potential companies.

The fund math behind generating fund returns

Portfolio construction goes hand-in-hand with fund math. Fund math refers to how the LPs and VCs will share in the profits made from company investments. LPs get paid for their investment in your fund if the value generated is greater than the dollars committed into the fund. The word "committed" is more relevant than "invested" because if one hundred million dollars is committed, LPs still have to pay fees on that capital. After fees, there may be only seventy-five million dollars to invest in companies, leaving the VC in a value hole. The only way to dig out of that hole is by generating significant value from the companies in which the VC is investing.

Every dollar put into a company, whether in the initial round or a follow-on round, should be carefully calculated because profits at the fund level are still calculated based on the one hundred-million-dollar commitment. A solid understanding of the underlying math that generates the value of the fund is important because it shows how you will make the money that flows back to LPs.

Fund math in venture capitalism relies on a power law curve of performance, which simply means a small number of your portfolio companies will deliver the bulk of your returns. The implication is that you should own a lot of each company up-front, but also that as companies progress, and you realize which companies are going to be the most valuable, that you put your follow-on dollars into these companies to deliver outperformance to your LPs.

Let's ignore gross and net returns in the following example for the sake of simplicity. As a VC with fund commitments of one hundred million dollars, you must generate three hundred million dollars in value to hit the desired return for an institutional LP. If you invest in a highly concentrated fund portfolio (say with ten companies), then this three hundred million dollars of value will be generated by only one or two of the companies. That is how venture capital works.

If you have ten companies in the fund, each with a ten million dollar cost basis—totaling one hundred million dollars in LP commitments—then each company should generate thirty million dollars of value back to the fund to reach a three hundred million dollar value. Venture capital, however, does not work perfectly. Most companies fail to achieve consistent returns, some companies will not return much beyond their cost basis, and a few will generate large returns, driving the overall returns of the fund. In this example, then, the ten million dollar investment would have to potentially yield two hundred or three hundred million dollars in value to deliver the LP an attractive return. LPs obsess about this math when considering a fund investment.

What are the key components of portfolio construction?

The building blocks of portfolio construction

- Fund size

- Number of companies

- Initial check sizes and ownership

- Reserves/follow-on check sizes and matriculation rates

- Valuation and other expectations

Each of these components affect the math of portfolio returns. Let's take a closer look.

Fund size: Once the fund is raised, it is a fixed number. The larger the fund, the more returns you will have to generate to have great performance. Smaller funds require less created value to generate great returns. That's why some small funds achieve very large multiples.

There are trade-offs between large and small fund sizes. For example, if you have a large fund, you can usually buy a company at the price you are willing to pay and get significant ownership in that company. If you have a small fund size, then you will not be able to pay higher prices and gain higher ownership.

Number of companies: Will you be investing in ten companies or a hundred? The expected number of companies will determine the initial check size per company and how much capital has to be reserved for follow-on rounds. A larger number of companies will translate into less capital being invested into a company, which, in turn, means a lower percentage of ownership. As a result, each company has to create significant value to individually affect overall fund returns.

LPs sometimes favor a "concentrated portfolio" because it means investing larger checks in a more manageable number of companies, as well as higher ownership in a smaller set of companies. This could equate to a greater pay-off overall, assuming a successful exit. For example, in a billion dollar exit, one percent ownership returns ten million dollars, which is not significant for a one hundred million dollar fund. However, ten percent ownership brings one hundred million dollars back, which means you have returned your fund. Anything beyond that sale is profit for you and the LP.

Initial check sizes and ownership: The larger the initial check size, or the smaller the valuation, the higher the initial ownership is. Ultimately, this results in a greater chance of returning significant capital to the fund during a successful exit.

The market usually determines valuation. The same size check that would have bought twenty percent of a company in 2010 only buys only ten percent in 2019. Thus, if that company is successful and sells for $1 billion dollars, you would receive only half the return because of the difference in market prices.

This indicates that initial ownership is important. Some VCs are flexible with initial ownership expectations and feel it is more important to have low ownership in a successful company than high ownership in a company that goes out of business.

If you know how many companies will outperform when you first invest, then ownership considerations probably don't matter. If you cannot predict the success rate at the onset (true for everyone I have ever met!), then optimizing ownership across the portfolio is a key factor in the decision-making process. Some funds are content with lower initial ownership in the first round of financing because they may get an opportunity to increase ownership in the strongest performers between rounds or during a subsequent round of financing (though admittedly this is difficult). Sometimes they gain access to super pro rata (buying up ownership in a subsequent round, or through secondary financing by buying shares from other investors).

Reserve ratio and "matriculation": How much capital have you reserved for your companies to invest in follow-up rounds, and how many companies can be expected to raise subsequent capital before selling or going public? In certain market environments, VCs may allocate capital at a faster than normal rate because:

(i) Many companies are raising subsequent capital sooner than expected. This includes pre-emptive rounds to avoid paying a higher price for the same company a few months down the road.

(ii) VCs are forced to invest reserves in subsequent rounds not originally anticipated. This can be driven, in part, by larger valuations generating larger pro rata allocations to the fund, making it desirable to buy more ownership or to prevent dilution. This can also mean averaging down returns on the initial invested capital. Having conviction in the portfolio's drivers early in the fund's life cycle is important when determining the best use of reserves.

Determining reasonable return expectations for successful companies: How easy or difficult will it be to sell your portfolio companies in the future? If the best companies are bought at reasonable exit expectations in a rational market based on appropriate comps, does this indicate that the fund is returning greater than three times net to LPs? Having reasonable return expectations and still showing a successful fund outcome is essential because the odds are that many companies will not achieve billion dollar-plus outcomes. An internal exercise can calculate the value needed for each company in the portfolio to return the fund.

How do LPs evaluate the investment terms of the fund?

The terms of the fund investment opportunity are provided in the pitch deck for the LPs to review. Terms that do not seem fair or that are generally "out of market" relative to other fund opportunities the LP is seeing can prompt the LP to pass quickly. If your goal is to reduce the number of factors that could cause LPs to pass quickly, then you need a good sense of market terms. Figure out what the current market terms are by talking to other VCs, LPs, or fund formation lawyers. Below are some common terms and some thoughts on how LPs might think about them. Note that these terms are defined in the previous chapter on the LPA.

- **Fund name and legal entity location**: If your limited partnership entity is based in an area that is restricted from investment by the LPs, then the LPs may simply have to pass because the fund is not a structural fit.

- **Investment objective**: Some LPs have mandates that restrict investing in certain strategies, such as public equities. If your investment objective includes investing in public equities, this would fall outside of the LPs' investment scope, and they might pass on investing in your fund.

- **Target fund size**: The smaller a fund is, the more attractive it is for producing a larger return on a multiple of capital basis. If the fund is too big, this may cause LPs to pass on the fund. On the other hand, a larger fund may indicate past success, and therefore give LPs *higher* confidence to invest. Context is key.

- **Minimum LP investment**: If you are working with smaller LPs, then having a large minimum investment check size can create a barrier for them when investing in your fund. The VC has discretion over who can invest and how much they can invest, meaning they can waive the minimum to bring valuable LPs into the fund.

- **Investment period**: LPs want to see a reasonable timetable for building a portfolio. The investment period for a normal fund is between two and five years.

- **Term**: The term is the life of the fund. Normally, venture capital funds in the U.S. run ten years with two one-year extensions. If your term is too short or too long, the LPs may not invest. If your term is too short, the assumption would be that there is not enough time to create value in private companies, or, if too long, the LP may decide that his/her capital will be locked up too long.

- **Venture capitalists' commitment (aka GP commitment)**: LPs want to see larger commitments by the VC to know they are dedicated to the success of the VC fund. Most VCs try to minimize commitment because their own cash is locked up. If the venture capitalist commitment is too small and there is not enough alignment between the VC and the ultimate returns of the fund, the LPs may pass.

- **Management fee**: Limited partners want to see a fair fee charged on assets under management (AUM). Venture capitalists will try to maximize this number, for example, because it could translate directly into larger salaries for them in the short term. If the management fee is too large, LPs may pass. On the other hand, if the strategy warrants higher fees, then LPs may believe the higher fees to be justified.

- **Preferred return**: This is not a very popular term, especially in the U.S. It is used more in regions such as Europe and may serve as a mechanism to make LPs comfortable with investing in a fund opportunity that will be actively managed to success.

- **Carried interest or incentive fee**: Like other fees on a LPs' invested capital, if it is too large, the LPs may elect to pass.

- **Fee offsets**: If you are charging management fees that adequately cover the operations of the venture capital firm, then any additional income you receive should be offset to the management fee. Make sure you understand fee offsets well.

What is an investment memo and why is it important for VCs?

An investment memorandum, or investment memo for short, is produced by LPs in preparation for meeting with their investment committee to solidify their understanding of the investment. If VCs write PPMs, it should be based on the idea that many sections will be pulled for the investment memo being crafted by LPs. VCs could write out key sections for the LPs in the PPM so it is easy to copy and paste the sections into the investment memo. However, as mentioned, PPMs in VC, especially early-stage VC, are rare.

The following is an example of sections of an institutional LP's investment memo with brief explanations about what the LPs are conveying to the internal team or investment committee for each section.

- **Executive summary of the investment opportunity**: Because of the volume of material to be read, the executive summary provides an overview of the investment opportunity. It gives a summary of what the fund does, what you will invest in, and a broad understanding of what the LPs like about the fund. Additional information can include the amount of capital the LPs recommend for investment and the timing of the fund close. If there is something different or materially significant about the fund, such as plans to bring on two new partners right after the first close, the LPs will highlight it in this section. This section may also include a summary of terms that are meaningful to the LPs return on the fund, and an extended summary of terms may be included in the appendix.

- **Key advantages to investing in the fund:** This section highlights the compelling reasons why the LPs want to invest in your fund. Key advantages could include a team that's been successful in the past at building a large technology company or generating significant investment performance with the expectation that this performance will continue.

- **Key risks to investing in the fund:** This section identifies the risk of the fund investment opportunity. A key risk could include a first-time fund manager because of the operational complexity of running a fund while also sourcing and investing in high potential teams and companies.

- **Team:** This section includes a quick summary of the investment team members and their backgrounds, especially as relates to the relevant networks used for sourcing investment opportunities. It includes those individuals who will source those investment opportunities. Extended biographies of key investment partners may also be included here or in the appendix.

- **Historical performance of the investment team**: This section includes the prior investment performance of the venture capitalists. A schedule of investments can be included here or in the appendix, which highlights the name of the investment, the amount of the investment, the amount realized, the current market value, the multiple of capital, and the other pieces of investment data that help LPs understand your portfolio, how you invest, and what you invest.

- **Investment strategy of the fund:** This section provides information on the investment strategy.

- **Market opportunity, especially as it relates to investment strategy:** This section discusses the fund investment in the context of the market. If you are a VC firm based in and investing in Israel, you could provide context on the Israeli investment market, including data on Israel investments, as well as information on what makes Israel a compelling market in which to invest, grow, and sell companies.

- **Investment process of sourcing and managing investments:** This section provides information on the investment process, including sourcing, conducting due diligence, the investment decision-making process, and managing and exiting investments.

- **Organization of the investment firm:** Organization refers to the broader venture capital team and can provide information about how the firm is structured. If the firm is the same team from another venture capitalist firm that is rebranding, that information could be highlighted in this section. Including an organizational chart is also important for larger teams.

- **Competition:** This section talks about what other VC funds you will be competing with for similar deals. If you are a seed fund specializing in financial services, you could be compared to other seed funds specializing in financial services. If you are a Series A fund that is more generalist, you may be compared to other funds of similar size investing similar amounts into similar companies.

What are additional sections found in an investment memo?

Organizational chart of everyone who works at the VC firm: For a larger venture capital firm, the LPs may include an organizational chart, especially if there are offices across multiple areas.

Biographies of the investment team: Extended biographies of key investment partners.

Schedule of prior investments and any investments in the current fund: A schedule of investments could include the name of the investment, the amount of the investment, the amount realized, the current market value, the multiple of capital, and the other pieces of investment data that help LPs understand your portfolio, how you invest, and what you invest.

Summary of fund terms: This section will include a brief discussion on the relevant terms that could affect the investment return for the LPs.

Case studies on the best performing companies from your track record: If you have invested in companies already, the LPs may include more information on a selected few of these investments to give other members of the LPs team an idea of the types of companies you have invested in and may invest in.

Limited partners (LPs) who are invested in the VC fund: This section is a list of other LPs invested in the venture capitalist fund.

What is quantitative due diligence?

Quantitative due diligence is a spreadsheet, document, or pitch deck created by LPs to assess your investment performance. For institutional LPs, this is a formal (and significant) part of the due diligence process. LPs gather investment data about your prior investment track record and portfolio companies; this information should be included in the data room so LPs can pull down the data to analyze and determine how well you have performed in the past.

In addition to looking at how you have performed on an absolute, stand-alone basis, the LPs will benchmark your performance against their existing portfolio, as well as market data benchmarks, such as Cambridge Associates, Preqin, or Oper8r. For LPs investing in multiple asset classes, you may also be compared to other asset class performances, such as public equities. If you have historical cash flows for prior investments, this can be done through a Public Market Equivalent, or PME analysis.

Quantitative due diligence is a significant part of the institutional due diligence process. Going into more detail is outside of the scope of this book.

Operational Due Diligence AKA Operations Review

What is operational due diligence ("O-D-D")?

Operational due diligence is the process by which LPs analyze the operational risks of a venture capital firm. If the VC does not run her/his firm well, then this can lead to lower returns for LPs. Therefore, institutional LPs consider the operational due diligence process as every bit as critical as investment due diligence. Typically, LPs will begin operational due diligence when they are interested in making an investment with the venture capitalist because it takes additional commitment of time and resources.

The VC should consider operational due diligence as a check-up on how well their firm is run. It is an opportunity to create accountability for maintaining the investment mandate and to reduce operational risks. The fact that LPs have come this far in the process is a positive sign.

Operational due diligence + first-time funds

It is important for first-time funds to make sure the operations of the firm are running smoothly (while carefully weighing a cost/benefit analysis with every operational decision in the early days). Having a well-run firm allows more time to make great investments and to generate higher returns. LPs will also look into the operations of the firm and how well the firm is being run as a sign of it being an institutional, long-term oriented VC which can lead to a higher probability of an institutional LP investing.

When LPs review the operations of the VC firm, they measure the risk of the VC's operations. How well is the VC running the firm? Has the VC set up a bank account and, if so, which bank, what is the reputation of the bank, where is it located, and is it familiar with how VC works? Did the VC put controls in place to accurately wire money to companies in a timely manner? Has the VC set up a valuation process to ensure accurate reporting to LPs? Running a venture capitalist firm is running a company. If a VC firm is not well run, it is high risk and more likely to fail. The LPs use the operational due diligence process as a chance to thoroughly review and scrutinize the processes and procedures of the VC to gain confidence in the fund investment opportunity.

What are the goals of operational due diligence?

The goals of operational due diligence are to assess the operations of the venture capital firm. The LPs expect the VC to be prepared to manage the business. This includes drafting policies that will keep the firm in compliance with regulations and hiring individuals or third parties to provide timely financial, auditing, and tax reporting. The LPs want to have confidence that you will be able to find and invest in great companies, and that you will be able to manage a firm.

What is an example of an operational due diligence process?

Operational due diligence can play out during due diligence in many ways. The LPs may have a separate process for reviewing the operations of your firm, which could include calling your Chief Financial Officer (or equivalent) and all of your service providers. The LPs may review your Due Diligence Questionnaire (the "D-D-Q") and determine that this review is sufficient to understand how your firm functions. Other LPs may not even ask these questions. The bottom line is—you want high returns and no loss on your capital.

A good operational due diligence process conducted by an institutional LP would go as follows:

- During due diligence, the LP would review all pertinent fundraising materials disclosed by the VC, especially the Due Diligence Questionnaire.

- The LP sets up a call with the VC with the intent of discussing the venture capital firm's policies and operations. Usually this call is between the LP and the CFO. But it can also be between the LP and the lead managing partner, or yet another member of the firm who has the most information on relevant operational topics.

- The LP has a conversation with the CFO asking clarifying questions about the DDQ or for additional information about the operations of the firm. If the VC has not disclosed items relevant for the LP to review, the LP should request these documents.

- The LP reaches out to the service providers that the venture capitalist works with to schedule and have a brief reference call.

- After gathering relevant information, the LP creates an operational due diligence memorandum, or "O-D-D" memo, and shares it with the investment committee. It is saved for future reference and could be iterated on a yearly basis, or at least every time a new fund is raised.

What topics do the LPs expect to review during the operational due diligence?

Operational due diligence can include a number of topics. At first glance, it can appear overwhelming because of this range:

- Valuation policy, including valuation methodology

- Accounting and reconciliation procedures

- Compliance (with regulations)

- Cash management

- Transaction controls

- Review of service providers

- Technology review (where and how the data is kept)

- Business continuity planning

- Counterparty risk management

- Management company information

What is a due diligence questionnaire and how can it help make fundraising more efficient?

One way to streamline operational due diligence is to write a due diligence questionnaire, referred to as a DDQ. This is a disclosure document written by the VC that answers many questions. If the VC does not write a DDQ, he/she will probably be meeting or taking phone calls from LPs to answer the same questions over and over. If the VC provides a DDQ as a disclosure document in the data room, then the LPs can review the document himself/herself. The DDQ should answer the majority of questions the LP may have. If there are additional questions after reviewing the DDQ, he/she can reach out with them.

Operational due diligence can be an intensive process. The DDQ streamlines this process by providing materials that review operational processes and procedures. While the DDQ will not encompass all the materials that could be disclosed during operational due diligence, it is a good document to answer common questions about the VC's operations.

What is included in a DDQ?

The DDQ can save time because the document is comprehensive and filled with a number of relevant sections. One of the top resources for a comprehensive DDQ is through the Institutional Limited Partners Association, or ILPA, an industry group that develops best practice materials for LPs.

A public use template developed by ILPA is available at the following URL:

https://ilpa.org/due-diligence-questionnaire/

Sections of a DDQ can include:

- General firm information
- General fund information
- Investment strategy and market opportunity
- Investment process

- Team

- Alignment of interest

- Market environment

- Fund terms

- Firm governance/risk/compliance

- Environmental, social, and governance (ESG) information

- Diversity and inclusion

- Track record

- Accounting/valuation/reporting

- Legal/administration

    ○ Data room service providers

    ○ Law firms

    ○ Consulting firms

    ○ Other third-party firms e.g., accounting, compliance

    ○ Background checks

- Technology review

Though not a fully comprehensive list, it covers the vast majority of essential questions that LPs review when assessing the operations of the VC.

What is an operational due diligence memorandum and why is it important for the VC?

The operational due diligence memorandum can be written as part of, or in addition to, the investment memo. An operational due diligence memo captures all the findings discovered during operational due diligence. It attempts to capture and assess any risks associated with the operations of the venture capital fund.

What do Lps do with the operational due diligence information after the fundraising process?

Lps review the operations of a VC firm during every fundraising cycle. Some Lps may ask for information regarding the operations of the firm when the venture capital firm is not fundraising. Be prepared to answer questions if any material changes are made to the firm's operations between funds.

Legal Due Diligence AKA Legal Review

What is legal due diligence?

During legal due diligence, the Lps review the legal risks pertaining to a venture capitalist investment. This process involves lawyers and can include reviewing the Limited Partnership Agreement and the subscription documents, as well as interfacing directly with the VC's lawyer. Legal due diligence allows the VC and Lps to discuss and negotiate the legal terms of the investment. This process is a necessary part of due diligence in advance of Lps making an investment.

When should you engage in legal due diligence?

Lps engage in legal due diligence if they are serious about investing in your fund. Hiring a lawyer is a testament to the Lps' confidence in the success of the fund.

On the other hand, a VC being open to negotiating with the Lps is an indication that the VC respects the feedback from the Lps and is open to negotiating terms. Sometimes negotiating will lead to changed terms, though it may not lead to any major changes. That usually depends on whether the VC or the Lps have more negotiating power. The Lps, of course, act in their best interest, and the venture capitalist will act in his or her best interest. This step should lead to the final terms and the legal contract that will govern the venture capital fund.

What are the goals of the legal due diligence process?

From the LPs' perspective, the goal of legal due diligence is an agreement on terms that are good for both the VC and the LP.

LPs' goals of legal due diligence:

- Review and assess the risks of the fund

- Review the LPA and come to an agreement that serves the long-term objectives of both the VC and LPs

- Decide on best terms that set up the VC fund for success

What is an example of a legal due diligence process?

- The VC prepares for a discussion with the LPs and talks with their lawyers to draft a Limited Partnership Agreement (LPA).

- The venture capitalist sends the LPA to the LPs to review.

- The LPs review the LPA with lawyers to generate comments on any terms that need clarification. LPs may either have lawyers in-house or use third-party law firms; for the VC, this would look no different. The LPs then send back the LPA comments to the VC for review.

- The VC processes the LPs' comments and does one of three things: accepts the comments, negotiates further with the LPs on certain terms, or rejects the LPs' comments.

- When all terms have been negotiated, a final draft of the LPA is signed by the VC and each LP. It then becomes the governing contract of the venture capital fund.

PHASE 3:
CLOSING THE FUND

CHAPTER 7

Building Your Limited Partner Base

The strength of the team is each individual member.
The strength of each member is the team.

—Phil Jackson

Introduction

When will LPs commit?

At some point, LPs commit to your fund. This could be verbal during a conversation at an annual meeting or in writing via email after a diligence meeting. As this happens, you gain momentum (especially if you can talk openly about LPs who have already committed), bringing you closer to your venture capital fund goal and target fund size. There is no set timeframe for when LPs will commit. A strong track record, a well-thought-out fundraising strategy, and demonstration that you are the right person to execute your strategy could bring a commitment in weeks—but it may also take months or years. However long it takes, a strong fundraising strategy that builds momentum is key to your success.

Deciding which LPs are appropriate for your fund is an important decision to make before you officially close the fund. You will have to decide which LPs are allowed to commit and what amount each one will contribute. Just as a CEO of a venture capitalist-backed company ultimately chooses investors, you, as a venture capitalist, get to choose your investors. The LPs that end up as investors in your fund are called your limited partner base, or LP base.

Definition of LP Base

The limited partner base, or LP base for short, refers to the group of LPs investing in a single venture capital fund. The LP base can be one investor investing in its own corporate venture capital strategy or multiple investors— up to hundreds of individuals and organizations—investing in your fund.

When choosing an LP base, look for distinct characteristics that make these LPs good investors and partners for the long term. For example, when you raise a venture capital fund, you are committing to at least ten years of fund management; your LP base should be willing to commit to the same timeline. How you choose your LPs, the characteristics of the LPs, and, consequently, the LP base you create, are important to you both as an individual and for the long-term success of your venture capital fund.

Building Your Limited Partner Base

How do you pick the right number of LPs?

There is no magic number for how many LPs should be in an LP base. There may be regulations that legally cap the number of investors you can have in your fund. In the United States, security laws, such as the Securities Act, Exchange Act, Investment Company Act, and the JOBS Act, govern the number of investors who can invest in your fund. All these acts have stipulations capping the number of investors you can legally accept into your fund, ranging from one hundred to an infinite number.

As the number of LPs you bring into your base increases, take into consideration how much time it will take to manage them. The higher the number of LPs, the more difficult management becomes. If, rather than executing your fund strategy and building your firm, you spend more time preparing disclosures and documents for review or traveling to limited partner meetings, you should reconsider who is invested in your fund and whether they should continue.

What are manageable numbers for an LP base? For institutional venture capital funds, the range most commonly cited is between ten and thirty core LPs. While the numbers are straightforward, the reality is, most first-time funds scrape and claw for many smaller checks. As a first-time fund, you do not have control over who invests and how much.

You do, however, have control over who you pitch to and how much you ask from those investors. For example, a high-net-worth individual may invest a quarter of a million dollars into your fund while an institutional LP might invest between one million to thirty million (20% of your fund). Most institutional LPs do not want to concentrate heavily into your fund, meaning going above an arbitrary percentage of the fund, usually between 10-20%. If you are raising one hundred and fifty million dollars, it would take a lot more pitching to high-net-worth individuals before closing the fund, so you should go after institutional LPs.

The number of LPs may differ depending on the size of the fund. For a fifty million dollar fund, you may need only a handful of institutional LPs, but the reality is, you will probably receive smaller checks when raising your initial funds and larger amounts as you become more successful. If you perform well, your initial LPs may commit more money as they see that you are performing well. This could result in fewer LPs over time.

You may be elect to winnow out some of the LPs who invested in your first-time fund. On the other hand, to maintain limited partner diversification, you may elect to bring on even more LPs in follow-on funds, ensuring that you are never overly reliant on any one LP in your LP base.

VC PERSPECTIVE FROM THE FIELD:
QUESTIONS TO ASK YOURSELF ABOUT NEW LPS

"How much money have they already invested in venture capital?

Which funds have they invested into in the past (and do they reference well as good partners)?

Will the LPs be active contributors in scaling your firm (more than just money)?

Do the LPs have the capacity to be long-term supporters of your firm?

Are the LPs aligned with your long-term vision and strategy?

Are you balancing the size of investors, not being overly dependent on one LP?[8]

Do you have a manageable number of LPs (e.g., 30-40 LPs) who make up the fund?[9]"

How do you size a limited partner allocation?

There are several issues to be aware of when sizing a limited partner position. The terms of the Limited Partnership Agreement (LPA) will define a minimum check size for LPs; this encourages LPs to invest if they are financially able and interested. Larger checks mean a faster close as well and are not much more work for VCs (in terms of logistics) than smaller checks. The VC can, however, accept smaller checks than the minimum—or they can also set up a parallel fund that accepts smaller checks. This type of fund may have different information rights and reporting requirements for those who cannot afford the higher minimums but nonetheless have a special relationship with the VC.

---

[8] If the LP has its own LPs. You are assessing the risk of the LP not being able to sustain their own business given unforeseen circumstances in their own LP base.

[9] Again, if the LP has its own LPs.

How should you think about an anchor LP check size?

If the VC is raising a fifty-million-dollar fund and a single limited partner wants to invest the entire fifty-million dollars, the VC could accept it. But most VCs would not accept this too-good-to-be-true offer because it would give that single limited partner too much influence over the fund. If that same limited partner decided not to invest in the next fund, it would leave a fifty-million-dollar hole in the LP base.

Then, the VC would have to start from scratch, re-building his/her LP base. This risk should be avoided. The goal is to have no LP with too large an investment. Your largest institutional LPs should have five to ten percent of the fund. No LP should commit more than fifteen to twenty percent of the fund because this could bring undue influence over how you invest and build your portfolio.

Here's another example, which is more nuanced. If you are now raising a fifty-million-dollar seed fund and you get a verbal commitment from the limited partner of twenty-million dollars, it comprises forty percent of the fund! On the one hand, this is great news: a twenty-million-dollar check into your fund is very attractive after you have been fundraising for almost a year! It moves you closer to your goal. You want to be done with fundraising as fast as possible so you can get back to investing in companies. Do you say yes? It depends.

There are additional considerations about the individual or organization behind the twenty million. Because all LP money is not fungible, you should know your relationship with the LPs, what benefit they bring to the fund, and other factors such as the LPs' network, brand, capital source, values, personality, and strategic goals before saying yes.

What do you do when you are oversubscribed?

Having to sort through which LPs get what allocations is a good problem to have! When you have more LPs interested in your fund than expected, be aware that you do not have to close on all of their capital. Closing on too much capital could change your investment strategy. For example, if you are raising fifty million dollars to invest in seed-stage companies and you close on two hundred million dollars, this would change your investment strategy, and you would probably have to invest in later-stage companies because your check sizes would be too large for seed-stage investing.

Tough decisions need to be made when allocating limited partner positions in the fund. Spend time deliberating on who you like, how the relationships will wear over what could be decades of investment partnership, and which partners will bring support to your own organization and, potentially, your portfolio companies.

Diversification And Key Characteristics

Why should a limited partner's personality and values be considered?

The relationship between you and the LPs is of paramount importance to the success of your venture capital firm. By raising a venture capital fund, you are embarking on a ten-year relationship with the LPs—indeed, a relationship that could last twenty or thirty years, or even until your retirement if you build a franchise that endures over multiple funds.

Spending time with the LPs and asking tough questions is a process of assessing their personalities and whether they will be good long-term partners. The LPs, too, will be assessing your personality and whether you have the determination to see your fund through to success. Be sure your values are aligned before taking any capital from LPs and becoming legally engaged in a partnership. Act with the absolute best intentions and integrity as you seek out LPs to work with you.

What does limited partner type mean?

LP type refers to the kind of investor from whom you are taking capital. There are many types of LPs, including banks, corporations, endowments, family offices, multi-family offices, fund-of-funds, foundations, high-net-worth individuals, insurance companies, sovereign wealth funds, pension funds, and other larger venture capital firms. There are other financial intermediaries, such as Outsourced Chief Investment Officers (OCIOs) and investment companies that manage and make investment decisions on the behalf of others.

Try to diversify your LP base by type, so no one partner has undue influence on you or the decisions governing the venture capital fund. You may notice that regulations, changes in strategy, liquidity needs, and the like drive changes in LP types over the course of building your firm. For example, in recent years, banks were faced with regulations reducing exposure to higher risk assets such as venture capital. Therefore, they became much less active in committing to venture capital funds.

LPs have different advantages and risks. Make sure you understand the advantages and risks of each LP before signing up for a long-term commitment with these individuals and firms.

Why is network an important factor when considering LPs?

Another way to think about LP diversification is the network each provides. The LP adds to the VC's existing network through the possibility of introductions to additional LPs, customers for portfolio companies, and even deal flow.

Why is brand and reputation important when considering LPs?

The LP's brand and reputation should not be overlooked. Ideally, the brand and reputation should be strong, thus attracting other LPs to look at your investment opportunity. Some LPs are known for selecting great funds and underwriting them with strong institutional investment processes. If there were risks to be identified, these LPs probably saw them and were comfortable with those risks before investing in you. These are the LPs you want because they send out positive signals to the rest of the market.

Why is source important when considering LPs?

If you are raising funds from a corporate limited partner that has slim margins for its business model, this may affect raising capital for subsequent funding, especially if its market has challenges. But if you are taking capital from an out-sourced chief investment officer (OCIO) whose clients are octogenarians, then those clients may diversify into more liquid assets. It is your role to identify the source of capital and think through how that source of capital may present an opportunity or a challenge in the future. Avoid wasting time with LPs that will never take on the risk of your strategy, or those that commit initially but will desert you in follow-on funds.

If you cannot identify where the LP's funds are coming from, this could also present a problem. Some family offices fail to disclose their benefactors, and this could be a red flag about accepting their capital. Always begin a partnership with a high degree of respect, transparency, and disclosure to secure a strong future relationship with the LPs. Think through the source of your capital and any implications. Then make a decision on your LP base.

Why is LP organizational structure important to consider?

As a VC, you will spend a considerable amount of time fundraising. Spend that time building a relationship with LPs that will serve as a long-term source of capital. Avoid rebuilding your LP base for every fund by accepting LPs with enough capital to invest in your current fund and enough capital to scale their LP allocation to invest in subsequent funds.

For example, institutional investors, such as endowments structured as long-term capital, are sometimes referred to as permanent capital. There is, however, no guarantee they will stay. Although the industry refers to them as permanent, a separate decision is made every time there is a follow-on fund, so you must perform well fund over fund. These types of LPs have formal and sometimes extensive fundraising processes where they review each fund's performance and make decisions based on the merits at that point in time.

Why is experience important when considering LPs?

It is desirable that the LP has experience investing in other venture capital funds, though it is not essential. To gauge an LP's experience, find out how many venture capital funds he/she invested in prior to your fund. Having past experience with other venture capitalists and understanding the characteristics of venture capital may indicate how knowledgeable the LP is and whether he/she can be helpful in building your firm. Expect these investors to offer expert opinions. The experience of the LP base will save you time by making your venture capital firm more efficient and better managed.

Find out how recently the LP invested in a venture capital fund. If the organization was investing in venture capital ten years ago and is just starting to get back into it, then its experience may be less relevant in the current venture capital ecosystem.

What is the limited partner advisory committee (LPAC) or advisory board?

A Limited Partner Advisory Committee (LPAC, colloquially pronounced the "El-Pack") is a subset of the LP base that advises the VC on matters such as conflicts of interest, valuation methodology, and other issues such as extending the investment period, extending the term of the fund, or approving investments that may fall outside of the strategy of the fund. The LPAC is composed of the largest (by check size) or most strategic LPs. If the LP is experienced, has a sense of best practices for managing a venture capital fund, and has a personality that you can work with over a long period of time, consider involving him or her in a more formal capacity.

Why should you think through the limited partner's strategy before taking capital?

Knowing the limited partner's strategy is important, and you should spend time thinking about how the potential partner's corporate and investment strategies align with your fund. For example, know whether the LP only invests in early-stage focused venture capital funds or prefers later-stage funds. If the firm only engages in venture investing in pre-Initial Public Offering (pre-IPO) companies, your early-stage strategy will not be a good fit. And unless the LP indicates explicitly that the firm is beginning a new strategy that aligns with yours, engaging in changing their minds is not a good use of your time. Being thoughtful up front about misalignment will save you time down the road.

Second, consider how many new managers the Lps invest in as opposed to how many established managers or "re-ups." If the LP invests in only one new fund per year after meeting with two hundred early-stage venture capitalists, the odds of being chosen are slim. But if the LPs are creating an emerging manager program and they invest in ten new venture capitalist funds per year, the odds improve for getting a commitment.

Third, think about whether your sector and geography are relevant to the LP. Has the LP invested in your sector before? Perhaps you are a healthcare fund, but the LP has never invested in healthcare and does not believe in the market's opportunity within venture capitalism because of very long enterprise sales cycles of healthcare customers. It is best not to pursue this LP.

Alternatively, maybe you are a Detroit-based venture capital firm investing in companies in Detroit and the Midwest. If the LP has never invested there before, then you should gain an understanding of why the firm would consider your fund at this time. Is there now an investment thesis that says Detroit is the next great technology development ecosystem and that your fund is poised to capture that opportunity? Be sure to have clear answers to these questions because they will affect how you manage the LP base.

Fourth, think about how LPs consider your fund strategy with respect to their own strategy. Strategic investing is when a corporation invests in a company or venture capital fund because it aligns with corporate strategy. The truth is, every good LP has an investment strategy, and your venture capital fund should fit into it.

Find out what motivates the LPs to invest in your fund. Is the LP a corporation trying to understand what technologies are being developed at the early stage within its market? Is the LP looking to broaden its exposure to venture capitalism and will it be a passive investor? Is the LP looking for co-investment opportunities? By understanding motives, you can assess whether a limited partner is a good fit, a process undertaken on a case-by-case basis. If the LP will not state directly what his/her strategy and motives are, then address any concerns early on with other VCs who have worked with the LP in the past.

CHAPTER 8

Negotiating The Limited Partnership Agreement And Side Letter

Building a visionary company requires one percent vision and 99 percent alignment.

—Jim Collins

The Final Approach To Closing The Fund: Executing The Legal Documents

What is important in negotiating the Limited Partnership Agreement and side letter?

It is imperative for both the LPs and VCs to negotiate well and be satisfied with the final outcome of the Limited Partnership Agreement. Both parties must aim towards negotiating a fair agreement that sets the basis for the long-term partnership.

The reality is that the LPA is a legal document and therefore contains confusing legal terms. Many of these terms are standard, meaning LPs have probably seen them many times before with other VCs. This is especially true if VCs elect to go with a "cookie cutter" LPA—a legal document that has been used in the past and offers terms favored by both VCs and LPs.

The LPA (and any additional terms put into a side letter) must be clearly defined so that the involved parties understand the agreed upon terms. Lawyers for both parties will be part of the negotiations, and the terms contractualized require a candid, tough discussion around the terms of the relationship.

How should the venture capitalist think about negotiating leverage?

Sometimes it is difficult to arrive at a fair deal if either party holds a majority of the power in negotiation. If this is the case, the power holder should consider the long-term success of the partnership, not the short-term. From the perspective of the VC, the LPs can influence the terms if they are meaningful investors and use this negotiating leverage to their advantage.

Experienced VCs know the terms relevant to LPs and negotiate these terms to a fair outcome. Less experienced VCs should get good advisors or experienced lawyers to offer advice as they negotiate to avoid running into structural issues that handicap the fund later. Lawyers are helpful in highlighting terms that need to be discussed—and perhaps changed—to avoid these potential issues.

What are best practices for negotiating a Limited Partnership Agreement?

Each limited partner has different priorities and therefore spends time on different terms. VCs can avoid challenges during this process by following these best practices:

- Best practices for negotiating a Limited Partnership Agreement begin with creating a negotiating plan. The VC should consult with his/her lawyer to decide what terms are most important, where to concede, and what terms are non-negotiable. Having this plan in place before engaging with the LP is critical.

- The LPs and VCs should both use lawyers to their advantage—again, not to compete and "win" the negotiation, but to arrive at a mutually agreed upon document that satisfies both parties. The right lawyer has extensive negotiating experience and simplifies the process by understanding specific fund formation terms.

- Be open to negotiating with more LPs than you may need as some may drop out even after they verbally commit to your fund.

- Transparency goes a long way toward building a strong foundation for a lasting relationship built on trust. Realize that even if your values are in the right place, others may not be as transparent as you or share your negotiating ethics. Be ethical, but also be cautious.

- Know when to walk away. This requires a good plan that defines what terms are important to you and what you cannot agree to.

- Build negotiating leverage. This is easier said than done, but if you understand the pain points and preferences of your prospective investors, you have more control than you might expect, even as a first-time fund.

- When moving through the logistics—the back and forth required for the negotiations—send redlines (which are the clauses of the LPA changed by lawyers which are tracked in red) to show what has changed. This saves time and streamlines the negotiation process.

LP PERSPECTIVE FROM THE FIELD:
THE IMPORTANCE OF CHOOSING A LAWYER

"Choosing a lawyer is the foundation upon which everything is built, and it is crucial to choose wisely. A good lawyer helps you with the timeline, understanding the variables, and developing the materials you will need.

There are two types of lawyers: entrepreneurial and accountant, with entrepreneurial being the preferred type. Entrepreneurial lawyers are practical and advise on when to raise funds from first and second degree connections. They will also advise on when not to spend extra money. Accountant lawyers tend to closely follow textbook strategies."

What terms should you focus on during the negotiation?

Terms can make or break a negotiation. If the VC and the LP do not agree on terms, then there can be no investment relationship. Therefore, it is important to discuss which terms are important at the onset and to make sure those terms (and the concerns that lie behind them) are properly addressed.

Theoretically, you could argue over every clause in the Limited Partnership Agreement, but this would be a drain on your time and would be unproductive. You are better off deciding which terms are materially important, prioritizing them, and negotiating to ensure you are satisfied with how they are structured. At the end of these negotiations, be certain these terms do not create a misalignment.

How could you, as the VC, lose negotiating leverage?

There are several ways to lose negotiating leverage. For example, your goal is to raise a twenty-five-million-dollar fund, and a LP offers to commit fifteen million to that fund. In this case, the LP would have influence over the terms in the negotiation. But, if you are a twenty-five-million-dollar fund, and an LP is only committing three million dollars, the LP can say what he/she believes to be fair terms but cannot influence the final terms.

As another example, if you do not have a differentiated strategy and a clear value proposition for LPs, you will lose negotiating leverage. If you have a strong proposition demonstrating sourcing, specialized expertise to help companies grow, or an economic structure that is more economical for the LP, then you have a fund product that could attract capital.

How should you, as the VC, think about negotiating with LPs to keep it simple?

My recommendation is that you treat any negotiation as another engagement in a long-term partnership. The goal should be to create alignment. As a VC, be sure to understand the motivation of the LPs and to seek clarity from them about anything that is not clear. For example, if LPs ask you to limit the types of investment securities you are considering, it may be because it creates adverse tax implications for them. If you are not aware of how your terms affect the LPs, just ask.

What is the summary of terms and why is it important during the negotiation?

The Limited Partnership Agreement can be very long, and to believe that each LP will read such a document full of legalese is aspirational. Be practical (and save legal costs) by creating a summary of terms before fundraising, which is a highly abbreviated Limited Partnership Agreement that gives partners a clear sense of what the general terms are. The main terms to be included are:

- Target fund size
- Investment strategy, e.g. venture capitalist, growth, etc.
- Security type
- Fee structure
- GP commitment
- Profit sharing

- Investment period (how many years will you invest)

- Partnership term (how many years will the fund last)

When you first draft your pitch deck and add a summary of terms, the Limited Partnership Agreement may not yet be written. Use the summary of terms to get feedback on what is acceptable to the LPs. The summary of terms is a first pass on what will eventually become the Limited Partnership Agreement.

What is the comment period?

During legal due diligence, there is usually a designated period when the VC requests feedback on the Limited Partnership Agreement (LPA). This is called a comment period.

This gives LPs an opportunity to formally provide feedback on the terms of the LPA. After creating the Limited Partnership Agreement with his/her lawyer, the VC will usually set a date—a few weeks or even months from when the LPA is released to the LPs. The LP then provides feedback to the VC on which terms are uncomfortable or need to be changed for legal reasons. The deadline for re-turning the LPA with comments is set by the VC.

To clarify the comment period even further, here is how it usually progresses:

1. The VC creates a draft version of the Limited Partnership Agreement with his/her lawyers.

2. The VC puts the Limited Partnership Agreement in the data room or sends it to the LPs directly, asking for comments and setting a due date for those comments to be returned.

3. The LPs review the LPA with their lawyers and draft comments to send to the VC. (If you have made it to this stage, you are very far along in getting an investment from the LPs.)

4. LPs will then send comments, usually through an e-mail, along with a redlined version of the Limited Partnership Agreement. This way, the VC can see what the LP has commented on or changed specifically.

5. The VC has the discretion to determine which comments to integrate into the final version of the Limited Partnership Agreement.

Sometimes this process is like a conversation between the LPs and the VC. The LPs submit comments, either to the VC or his/her lawyer (or both), and then the VC responds. There may be a few back and forth comments, all with the intention of arriving at agreement on terms that concern the LPs that the VC can adjust.

Sometimes LPs simply submit comments to a "black box" and do not see how they are received or integrated until the final version of the Limited Partnership Agreement is released. This is not necessarily good. Attempt to create alignment with your LPs; creating the final version of the Limited Partnership Agreement without a conversation that addresses the fundamental concerns of Limited Partners may damage your relationship with them.

Sometimes the VC does not share the LPA with all LPs to start. Usually, the anchor LPs in the fund see it first. These LPs may have extensive experience in helping to draft a Limited Partnership Agreement that is fair and viable for themselves, while not discouraging the VC. Being able to convince LPs that have "been there, done that" to invest may work in your favor. It signals to other potential investors that the Limited Partnership Agreement has been professionally reviewed. As it costs LPs money to review an LPA, this may persuade potential partners with smaller amounts to invest—and who, thus, could not spend money on reviewing the agreement—to join the fund.

The Side Letter

What are side letters?

Side letters are legal agreements in the form of a letter with one or more additional terms not included in the main Limited Partnership agreement. Side letters are common in the legal due diligence process and many LPs request them. While VCs are not obligated to provide side letters, they are sometimes necessary. They might be called for, for instance, when a pension fund needs certain legal disclosures, or for negotiation purposes with an anchor LP.

Side letters exist because at least one LP wants additional terms not defined in the terms of the Limited Partnership Agreement. Side letters benefit LPs who are asking for a term not defined in the LPA. Sometimes LPs ask for side letters because they have enough leverage to demand certain terms, especially if they are very large investors. Other times, LPs may have their own regulatory requirements or commitments to its own investors.

How do side letters differ from the Limited Partnership Agreement?

Side letters are requested in addition to the terms defined in the Limited Partnership agreement. They are provided to LPs by the VCs as an add-on so the Limited Partnership Agreement itself does not need to be changed. A VC does not need to provide side letters.

Should the venture capitalist use side letters?

Side letters can include anything from discounted management fees to additional information disclosures by the VC.

LP PERSPECTIVE FROM THE FIELD:
THE NECESSITY OF SIDE LETTERS

"A side letter is the most convenient place to address special tax and regulatory needs of institutional LPs. Side letters can also work to a VC's advantage if he/she isn't ready or willing to go through an amendment process for a term not of interest to other investors, or one that clarifies a term for a particular investor.

Side letter terms can be economic or non-economic. Without over-generalizing, non-economic side letter provisions, when used judiciously, are appropriate. The subject becomes more nuanced when VCs—generally VCs with less bargaining power—must choose between creating economic inequities among LPs or risk the loss of a significant investment. Side letters, as with every other provision governing the relationship between the VC and the LP, are subject to a straightforward risk/reward analysis."

Can the risk of creating terms more beneficial to one investor be worth the risk of alienating other existing (or future) investors? If disclosed, will those partners reinvest in a subsequent fund? Will they organize and demand the same terms as a group? What is the harm to the sponsor's reputation? Is there a real or perceived conflict of interest that would give rise to a claim by the investors?

The potential reward is that investors seeking special provisions may offer something truly substantial to the fund: an early, large commitment; sufficient capital to make the entity viable; proprietary relationships within a critical ecosystem, or guidance for a new team. Providing special rights to some can offer real benefits to the whole. And if the beneficial rights are in a side letter, the sponsor does not have to start fundraising for his/her next fund by negotiating out of terms in the partnership agreement for a previous fund.

How do you compose the side letter?

Before drafting a side letter, consult your lawyer and discuss the terms to be included. If the terms can be included in the Limited Partnership Agreement, then include them there to save time and money, rather than drafting a separate side letter. Simplify the number of documents that govern the relationship between the VC and LPs.

What is the most favored nation clause?

A most favored nation clause is commonly found in side letters. It extends preferential terms negotiated by some LPs in a separate side letter to other LPs. This clause is an attempt to make the additional terms fair across the LP base. Understand this clause well and its potential implications!

CHAPTER 9

Logistics Of Closing A Venture Capital Fund

If people like you, they'll listen to you, but if they trust you, they'll do business with you.

—Zig Ziglar

Introduction

What is next?

Over the course of fundraising, you have faced many challenges. You started with the concept, established an investment strategy, met LPs who said "no" and many who said "yes," which has led to verbal commitments from these LPs. You are now ready to wrap up the fundraising process.

It is time to meet again with your lawyers to ensure all the closing documents are in order, including the Limited Partnership Agreement, any side letters, and the subscription documents. When your lawyers give you the green light, you can set a closing date for the fund.

You might wonder what is meant by "closing the fund." Closing of course does not mean to shut the fund down! On the contrary, closing means due diligence is complete, terms have been negotiated between the LPs and VC, LPs are convinced to invest, and they are ready to enter a legally binding partnership entrusting you to invest their capital. The process of entering into that legally binding partnership with the LPs is to "close the fund."

LPs commit to the fund by sending in legal agreements, sometimes called subscription agreements, subscription documents, or "sub docs." The lawyers review all the materials again to ensure everything is in order before "closing the fund." When the fund is closed, the venture capitalist can legally begin investing the capital into companies.

What is the typical process for closing a venture capital fund?

Closing involves the LPs who verbally committed to the fund and the fund lawyers who process the completed subscription document. The lawyers gather all the necessary documents from the LPs (primarily subscription documents) and send out a final email to all LPs that includes the final allocation and size of fund.

What does it mean to close your fund?

Closing a fund refers to the time when the VC has collected commitments from LPs and, with legal assistance, officially sets up the fund with the LPs' committed capital.

LP PERSPECTIVE FROM THE FIELD:
ADVICE ON WHY TO STAY ORGANIZED AND COORDINATE

"Smaller VC funds have individual LPs with busy lives and multiple priorities. Larger funds have larger LPs with institutional hoops to jump through prior to close. With that in mind, there is no replacement for having all oars in the water.

Fundraising is a high touch process, even when the VCs have deep and enduring relationships with prospective LPs. If the entire team is focusing 80 percent of its time and energy on ready closers and 20 percent on the next most promising group, it can provide that high touch that helps transition investors from "unfocused" to "subscription submitted."

Secondly, it is critical to coordinate with the legal team shortly before the final push. At the end, they should be standing by to help resolve any investor concerns. They can also contact investors to check the status of subscription agreements and review them immediately upon receipt for any incomplete items.

As part of that teamwork, set up a shared spreadsheet—not just for the lawyers, but for the whole team. Use it as a living document to know the status of every prospective investor in real time. Who is in? For how much? Was their wire received?

Speaking of wires, and maybe it goes without saying, keep the wire instructions clean and easy to follow. An individual should be able to wire from his or her home computer without calling the VC or its service providers because the wire instructions are too complicated."

Why do you need to close your fund?

You need to close the fund before you start investing in companies with the committed capital. Closing a fund is the necessary final step to use the capital invested by the LPs.

When do you close your fund?

The VC decides when to close the fund. He/she sets a closing date by which time all LPs' paperwork must be submitted.

The first close happens when you have enough committed capital from LPs to execute your strategy. Decide if you have enough "soft circled" capital, an industry term meaning that LPs have verbally committed to investing in your fund. The LPs are now ready to legally close so that you can use the capital for investments.

Sometimes the timing of the fund closing will not be up to you. LPs will probably have an opinion about the right amount of capital for your fund to execute. The LPs commit to your fund under certain conditions, including the subscription agreements, which are kept in escrow until you reach a given level of committed capital. The LPs decide when the committed capital is large enough to execute your investment strategy. Most LPs do not want to be the first to commit because they fear being the only one committed.

How do you decide on a first close date?

You may have only one close, though this will probably not be the case if you are raising your first venture capital fund. This first close date is arbitrary. Choose a date convenient for you and for the LPs, giving them ample time to engage with you during due diligence, to build a working relationship with you, and to be able to work through the legal documentation review.

This may take up to several months or even years. When the decision on a close date is made, tell the LPs so they can develop their own calendars for the diligence process and can allot resources to meet the deadline. Setting a close date improves the chances of having an efficient process with the LPs.

How do you close your fund?

There are three ways to close a fund. In the first way, the VC closes on the capital all at once in a process known as "one and done."

In the second way, the VC holds multiple closes over time, setting up a schedule conveyed to the LPs. This is usually done by VCs with a good sense of how much capital they can raise who need to give some LPs more time for due diligence and submitting the necessary documentation to invest in the fund. It is also done out of necessity by the VC so he/she can close on part of the capital and begin investing.

The third way allows a VC to have rolling closes whenever there is a new commitment from an LP. The logistics of a rolling close benefits the VC, but it ensures that LPs can commit as they become interested. Thus, they do not have to wait until there is an interim close.

One-and-done

The venture capitalist closes the fund in one session with all commitments completed on one closing date. The LPs are able to go through the diligence processes quickly and make a commitment. One-and-done fund closes are popular with LPs when the investment opportunity is obvious.

The LPs expect all diligence—operational and legal—to be complete. All legal documents, including the Limited Partnership Agreement, subscription agreements, and any side letters, will have been submitted. Limited partners may ask for an exception to a one-and-done close if they have enough leverage or if they wish to commit but cannot yet structurally invest.

For example, perhaps an endowment has reached its maximum commitment amount for the year and the final close is at the end of December. The endowment may then be allowed to come in January after the final close when the next annual investment budget is set. If the endowment has an investment meeting on July 1 and the close is set for June 30, the VC can be flexible with the close. Though it is not preferred by the VC, it can be done in exceptional circumstances.

Multiple closes

A VC may decide to hold multiple, predefined closes over the course of the fund-raising process if there is enough investor interest to hold a first close. This first close does not get the VC to the target fund size or the hard cap, so fundraising continues with subsequent pre-defined closes until the goal is reached.

Multiple closes can be done by VCs who want to start investing as quickly as possible. Holding a close gives the VC the legal right to call the capital and begin investing. Given that it may take months or even years to complete fundraising, being able to hold an interim close is important to remaining relevant in the market.

Multiple closes can be risky for the LPs if the VC closes on too little capital for his strategy. LPs may then be locked up in a fund that cannot perform its original strategy. If the LPs are not confident of your fundraising success, they may not deliver legal documents required to close until they know there is enough capital to execute. Many LPs will be conservative, but there will be some convinced enough to commit the first check for a first-time fund. Capital invested during and after the initial close has an interest fee that can amount to hundreds of thousands of dollars for large, active investment funds.

Rolling closes

Sometimes a VC does not set specific target closing dates, but rather will accept subscriptions agreements on a rolling basis as LPs commit to the fund. This is different from multiple closes when the venture capitalist decides to have a pre-defined number of closes and all LP documentation is due on those specific dates.

Reducing risk for the prospective LP buyers

Sometimes LPs may want to place investment documents in escrow. For example, an LP can submit all of his/her legal documents, adding a restriction preventing the VC from closing the fund until at least one hundred million dollars in capital commitments have been obtained from other LPs. When the VC collects all commitments, then the original investment can get out of escrow.

Who is involved in closing your fund?

The VC, the LPs, and the lawyers for both parties are the players involved in closing the fund. The VC will send the LP subscription documents that have been drafted and approved by the VC's lawyer. The LPs review, fill out, and send back all signed documents to the venture capitalist and his/her lawyers. The lawyers process all of the documents and officially close on the fund.

What are tactics for getting to a first close?

Getting capital from investors is challenging. Sometimes it may require providing the right incentive to get investors to commit. There are several time-tested tactics you can consider to get to a first close, including:

1. Leveraging an existing relationship to secure an anchor investor

2. Discounting fees or offering other attractive terms for early investors

3. Creating scarcity value for your fund; most LPs desire something they believe is in high demand

Again, the goal is to secure an initial amount of capital. The saying goes, "Beggars can't be choosers," but you can be clever. The reality of fundraising is that getting to that first close is one of the most challenging times in the lifecycle of a fund. Being open minded may help achieve that first close.

What if you don't close on all of the capital in the first close?

Many venture capitalists do not close all the capital at once. They hold multiple closes before getting to their target fund size and stopping the fundraising process.

The dual role of investing and fundraising

Once there are enough commitments for a first close, there is a transition from fundraising to investing. Venture capitalists prioritize differently—some may continue to spend the majority of their time fundraising, and others spend more time investing with the capital committed. Still others may balance both. This is easier if there are multiple partners with one partner managing the fundraising. If you are raising a fund alone, you have to assume two jobs—fundraising and being a full-time investor.

Stay on strategy during your initial investments

Some LPs do not invest in first closes. They like to see how the fundraising plays out with the intention of investing later in the fundraising cycle. They sometimes miss the fund entirely.

These LPs may already have a venture capitalist portfolio and will selectively add new managers, thus having the luxury of waiting to invest. To persuade these more conservative LPs, you must show that you have sound judgement and can stick to your investment strategy. If you are an AI-focused fund, invest in AI companies. If you are a seed stage fund, make seed stage investments. If you do not invest in what you say you're going to invest in, LPs may question your judgement and view you as high risk.

When do you stop fundraising?

Legally, fundraising has to stop after a defined length of time. Usually, VCs have twelve months to eighteen months after the initial close to keep fundraising.

Technically, the venture capitalist can ask for an extension, though it requires cost and approval from existing LPs.

Given the stress and dedication involved in raising a fund, you probably do not want to continue fundraising for another year after your first fund. It may make more sense to give yourself a hard deadline. When you reach that deadline, close on any new commitments. Whatever you have at that date, make do with the amount and invest it. If it is smaller than expected, you will probably come back to the market sooner anyway, so there is no gap with your investments.

When is it time to stop bringing in new LPs?

The point of fundraising is to build strong relationships with all LPs, and you should meet with prospective LPs whether you are fundraising or not. However, during fundraising for a first-time fund, especially when engaging with LPs is known to take longer to reach a decision, you should be transparent about the timing for your fund close.

If an LP takes four months to complete due diligence and then has to meet with an investment board every quarter, the timing to get to a decision could be almost seven months. If you expect to stop fundraising after three months, you should explain this to the LPs and see if it still makes sense for them to engage in the process. It is probably not a fit for the current fund unless something can be changed in the LPs' due diligence process.

How to think about your "hard cap."

A "hard cap," defined as the maximum amount a venture capital fund can raise, is set by the VC in the LPA. The hard cap indicates to LPs how much you will raise as a maximum, giving the LPs parameters within which to understand your investment strategy. Similar to setting you target fund size, setting your hard cap is an exercise in thinking through how much capital makes sense for your investment strategy.

For example, if you are an early-stage fund with a fifty-million-dollar hard cap, you will probably be a seed investor when you are fully raised. However, if you are raising fifty million dollars and don't have a hard cap, you might end up raising two hundred million dollars because of past success and therefore high demand from LPs. Then it would be harder for you to implement your original strategy of seed investing.

You would have to write larger checks and your strategy would change to later-stage company investments. The LPs originally invested in what they thought to be a fifty-million-dollar fund. Instead, they would now be stuck with a fund investing in later-stage companies. A hard cap can help solve some of these issues.

After a first close, some LPs, including institutional investors such as pensions and foundations, will begin to take you more seriously. There is sometimes a behavior of ensuring the fund will be successful in raising the fund before leaning in to engage. If you have attracted "high conviction" smart investors early on in the fundraising process, other LPs may follow.

Subscription Agreement

What is a subscription agreement?

A subscription agreement is a limited partner's application to become an investor in the venture capital fund—similar to applying to a college, for example, LPs apply to become investors in the venture capital fund. Subscription agreements capture lots of standard information, such as name and address of the prospective LPs, whether they qualify as accredited investors, how much the LP would like to commit to the venture capital fund, and other important information.

Who creates the subscription agreement?

Lawyers are responsible for creating the subscription agreements. While Limited Partnership Agreements (LPA) can change based on the terms negotiated between the LP and the VC, subscription agreements do not change. They are simply filled out by the LP as part of the process for becoming an LP in the fund.

Who fills out the subscription agreement?

The LP, or his/her lawyer, fills out the subscription document. For regulatory reasons, it is important that the information entered into a subscription document is accurate.

Where do the LPs send the subscription agreement?

Once an LP has finished filling in a subscription agreement, the completed subscription document is sent to the VC and his/her lawyer.

What should the VC think about before accepting the limited partner into the fund?

The VC gets to decide who will become a LP and how much each LP can commit. For example, an LP may enter a twenty-million-dollar commitment. However, if the VC is only raising thirty million, then she/he may not want such a large check from one LP.

The VC has to think about how much influence he/she is giving to the LP. The LP, in this case comprising two-thirds of the fund, would have undue influence over the venture capitalist. Personally, I invested in a thirty-five-million-dollar fund and there was another limited partner who wanted to invest the full thirty-five million dollars, given the reputation and performance of the venture capitalist. The venture capitalist did not accept the subscription for thirty-five million dollars, and the largest check in the fund was only five million. I have seen other VCs take the full amount, though, if the relationship with the LP is strong enough.

When does the fund actually close?

The fund closes when the LP is accepted in the venture capital fund. The lawyers for the VC send a letter informing the LP of the acceptance and the amount of the commitment.

When can the VC make the first capital call?

Once the fund has closed, the VC can make the first capital call, which the LP is legally obligated to pay within ten business days.

PHASE 4:
LP RELATIONS &
RAISING THE
NEXT FUND

CHAPTER 10

Managing The Limited Partner Relationship After Closing The Fund

Excellent firms don't believe in excellence—only in constant improvement and constant change.

—Tom Peter

Introduction

What happens when closing a venture capital fund?

Your fundraising is done—now what? Closing a venture capital fund begins the continuing relationship between VC and LP. Even though the Limited Partnership Agreement legally governs the relationship between you and your LP, at the heart of this relationship is trust-building, pragmatism, and respect.

Closing the fund is a big accomplishment. It is time to invest the committed capital and to foster a relationship with the limited partner. Once you close your fund, follow these best practices for engaging with LPs:

1. Clarity, consistency, and candor are the recipe for success to ensure a long-term source of capital.

2. As a Menlo Park-based managing director of a top-tier fund noted: "Our best practice would be to never make fundraising feel like a distinct period—so long as you're regularly updating your Limited Partners on the fund's investments and strategy, it should be a seamless process."

3. Remain open-minded about prospective Limited Partners. If an LP said no to your current fund, he or she might still invest in your next fund. Make sure you establish a means of staying in touch with him/her before the next fundraise. The relationship with prospective LPs must remain active. By maintaining a high degree of transparency, you help to build trust.

4. LPs spend much time monitoring existing investments. Making this easier helps LPs stay abreast of how your portfolio of company investments are performing. Define fund-reporting processes and what information you share with LPs so they can measure and track your progress.

LP Engagement And Communications After The Close

What information disclosures and timing do LPs prefer?

The answer depends on the LPs, but they all should be kept informed on a regular basis and in a timely manner. There is that fine line between too little information and too much. Communicate effectively and always remember that transparency is key.

VC PERSPECTIVE FROM THE FIELD:
EFFECTIVE WAYS TO SHARE INFORMATION WITH LPs

"We have made it standard practice to share an investor update with our entire LP base every eight weeks. We normally advise startup founders to do this, so we decided we should do the same. Typically, we share standard metrics such as TVPI, percentage of the fund invested, and the like . . . as well as some commentary related to specific companies, our firm, or the market at large. We welcome feedback and are available to dig into details or to answer follow-up questions, but generally, we try to steer our LP base around these updates [in terms of providing them with all of the information they would need to properly monitor our fund and its underlying company investments].

For our Limited Partner Advisory Committee (LPAC) specifically, we also make regular calls, usually monthly or quarterly. This is when we can go a bit deeper into specific topics with our most trusted advisors and largest LPs and can also dig into particularly sensitive topics that we do not want to put in writing for our general bi-monthly LP updates."

There may be terms you committed to in the Limited Partnership Agreement obligating you to share information at specific times, such as in quarterly financial statements. These statements are shared one-hundred-and-twenty days after the quarter closes. Audited financial statements, on the other hand, are shared within ninety days after your financial year. Send only what is asked and always use best practice.

In addition to the Limited Partnership Agreement, you may have side letters with LPs that require additional disclosures at specific times. Be sure to meet these demands.

Sharing information and doing it in a timely way strengthens relationships with LPs and provides them with more insight into the fund's progress. Having informed LPs helps during times of duress or ambiguity. Keep LPs briefed on organizational and portfolio developments. Be transparent and build trust.

Ask the LPs what information disclosures and timing they prefer and determine if you can meet their requirements without creating a burden on your internal resources.

Quarterly letters provide clear updates on the team, organization, and portfolio companies. Disclose information clearly in your financial statements.

An annual letter provides insights as to your thoughts on the market and portfolio companies, demonstrating your commitment to creating value in your portfolio.

Meet with LPs several times each year. One of these meetings should be an Annual General Partner Meeting (AGM). At this meeting, provide LPs with updates on your team, strategy, and portfolio. LPs need to keep track of your performance over time, and staying connected by being transparent with developments helps lighten the burden on them and makes you top of mind.

What happens after the fund closes?

Staying in touch with the LPs and communicating on a regular basis is very important. Limited partners want transparency, consistent communication, and advance notice of anything that might require their attention as they now monitor your fund as part of their broader investment portfolio. If the LPs have not heard from you for a while, and you then alert them of something that needs immediate attention, they may feel forced to make a decision too quickly and this may not bode well for the strength of your relationship with them.

VC PERSPECTIVE FROM THE FIELD:
ADVICE ON TURNING YOUR FUND INTO AN ENDURING BRAND

"Because most venture firms return to the fund-raising circuit for fresh capital every several years, structurally they are not 'enduring' firms. Investment banks, operating companies, and most corporate entities are permanently capitalized and endure as long as their revenues exceed their expenses. But most venture firms "meet their maker" about every three years. So the most challenging part of building an enduring brand IS repeated, consistent, fund-to-fund success."

What happens if the LP did not invest in this fund close?

The LP is investing in you and needs to build a personal relationship before making an investment. Having time to understand your personality, habits, and future potential makes sense, especially if you do not have an investment portfolio with a proven track record. If the LP did not invest in this fund close, make sure you are highlighting information that can assist them with making a more informed decision on your fund. Additionally, perhaps refrain from *only* asking them for money, understand what they need help with, and be helpful in the interim in the spirit of building the relationship in advance of an investment into your fund.

How often should you meet with LPs?

It is recommended that you have at least two meetings a year with each of your LPs. Focus on providing an update and answering questions on anything related to the fund or firm. Give them an opportunity to ask questions to help them understand how you are building your organization and portfolio.

How should you discuss difficult topics with LPs?

Do not ignore your LPs, connecting only when something has gone wrong or when you are kicking off a new fundraising process. Establishing appropriate channels of communication and building a good relationship—based on fairness and developing value—will ease difficult conversations.

What Are Specific Ways A VC Interacts With An LP?

Firstly, what is legally defined in the Limited Partnership Agreement and side letters about interacting with LPs?

Many times, the Limited Partnership Agreement and side letters will define the information rights of the LPs. The LPA and side letters tell you how often you have to tell your LPs about what you are doing and what information must be disclosed. These are legal requirements if the terms are in the LPA or a side letter.

The VC is legally obligated (by the LPA) to send a quarterly update within ninety days from the end of the quarter to the LP. Many VCs also hold quarterly calls to review the quarterly letter and offer additional context on organizational or portfolio updates. By hosting a conference call with LPs, the VC can control what the LP focuses on and can answer questions the LPs may have about the portfolio, strategy, organization, or market.

How do you stay in touch with LPs?

The VC is responsible for staying in touch with the LP. The aforementioned quarterly letters can include details on substantive changes to the organization, progress of portfolio companies, and valuation changes to the fund.

What are quarterly letters?

Quarterly letters are required by the Limited Partnership Agreement. They are a form of disclosure to the LPs, so they can monitor their investments. These can be written in many ways and include sections on such things as organizational changes, adding a new team member, company updates (such as a new product release or new customer acquisition), and valuation changes (such as when a portfolio company sells to a strategic buyer).

Some VCs become known for their high-quality quarterly letters, and LPs look forward to their commentary and insights. A well-written quarterly letter builds a relationship with the LP by giving him/her insight into how the VC thinks.

You can also use your quarterly letter to inform prospective LPs of your firm's progress. Given constraints on your time, this is a "write-once-share-many" strategy that makes the work invested in creating the quarterly letter go the extra distance. Some VCs post these online on their blogs or websites. You will already be putting significant time and thought into communicating with existing LPs, so be sure to share your perspective with others if it helps build your firm.

What are quarterly calls?

A quarterly call, which is a conference call with all the LPs, is recommended but not required. It provides another way to communicate with the LP and compounds the meaningful relationship you want to build. One way to structure the call is to follow material included in the quarterly letter. If there is any confusion, LPs can then ask questions to clarify firm and fund developments.

What is the annual meeting?

Annual meetings, also referred to as Annual General Meetings or AGMs, are yearly gatherings organized by the VC to bring together the VC, existing LPs, prospective LPs, and the VC's portfolio company CEOs. This is sometimes a formal meeting required by the Limited Partnership Agreement, during which the VC gives the LPs a thorough update on the portfolio, investment strategy, and firm.

As the VC, you should treat the AGM as an opportunity to inform your LPs of positive developments at your organization. You can also highlight any concerns you may have, and the AGM provides a forum to talk through these concerns.

The following questions should be discussed during the annual meeting:

- How is the portfolio performing?

- What new companies have you invested in since the last annual meeting?

- Are there any significant developments in the market you are investing in—for example, healthcare technology or life sciences?

- Are there any changes to the investment strategy?

- What is the reasoning behind any large strategy or organizational changes?

- Who are the key new hires at the venture capital firm?

- Are there any upcoming fundraising plans?

Answering the above questions can provide structure for the meeting. Many times, when providing information and insight into the portfolio, the venture capitalist has CEOs present their companies. The LPs then get to learn about the companies that their dollars are financing.

The annual meeting also serves as an opportunity for the LP to connect with the CEOs, which many find important because it demonstrates that the VC has strong relationships with the CEOs. LPs want to know if the VC has partnered with best-in-class founders who are building game-changing companies and whether he/she is maintaining these relationships.

While the agendas for these meetings vary by individual VCs, most will resemble this sample:

- Registration

- Presentation by the fund's investment team, including answering the above questions

- Presentations by CEOs, who talk about their respective companies

- Dinners are usually held on nights before or following the AGM to facilitate conversations among VCs, LPs, and founder CEOs. Having a fluid conversation during the AGM, especially in a more relaxed setting such as a dinner, is an efficient way for LPs to understand the portfolio.

AGMs also provide another opportunity to engage with prospective LPs. Sometimes LPs do not have a strong enough relationship with the VC, do not understand the strategy or portfolio, or need more time to understand how committed the VC is to the long-term success of his/her portfolio. An AGM offers a chance to show prospective LPs how much passion and work you are putting into building your firm.

There are other creative ways to use the AGM to expand your network and benefit your portfolio companies. For example, you can invite prospective follow-on investors to your portfolio companies or invite customer prospects to your AGM.

How often should you meet with LPs committed to your venture capital fund?

VCs should meet with LPs routinely in person, perhaps twice a year if possible. During these meetings, the VC and the LP can talk about updates to the organization, strategy, and portfolio. Both parties should set an agenda so the meeting is conducted efficiently. Agendas can be exchanged beforehand by email, allowing both parties time to discuss matters important to them.

A letter and a sample agenda for an ad hoc meeting could look something like this:

"Hi Winter,

Great seeing you at a technology conference last week. I hope your panel went well.

I am looking forward to our meeting next week. My thinking is we could cover the following topics:

1. Introduce Ann, our newest partner, who joined from this great financial services company where she led the data science team

2. Update on our latest investments, including a seed investment in Company A that we closed on last week (and have yet to announce publicly)

3. General market update, including changing competitive dynamics we are noticing and how we are adapting our strategy to the increased interest in our area of focus

4. Timing update on our next fund

Please let me know if there are any other items you would like to discuss.

See you next week,

Jennifer"

To manage risk, LPs have an obligation to check in on a regular basis with the VC about the operational side. The LP should review the portfolio disclosures sent every quarter, as well as audited financial statements sent at the end of the financial year.

As the VC, hiring a third-party independent auditor is a cost but is an important factor. Audited statements are considered an accurate assessment of the financial performance of the fund, and LPs prefer this added layer of oversight. Audited statements can be essential for smaller funds, especially if the limited partner requires them to invest in your fund.

Engaging Your Limited Partner Advisory Committee (LPAC)

What are Limited Partner Advisory Committee meetings?

If you have a LPAC (remember, "El-Pack")—sometimes (incorrectly) referred to as an Advisory Board—then use it. Venture capitalists should host at least two LPAC meetings a year, or whenever there is a pressing need to discuss substantive issues that directly affect the venture capital firm.

To make the number of meetings and travel manageable, one of these meetings can coincide with the venture capitalist's annual general meeting (AGM). The venture capitalist could host a special dinner the night before the annual general meeting for the LPAC members, or, alternatively, the venture capitalist could have the LPAC members stay for a lunch session after the annual meeting's main presentation.

How do you use the Limited Partner Advisory Committee to your advantage?

If no formal LPAC meeting is scheduled, bring it together as the need arises, especially when making key decisions and material changes to the organization or strategy. An ad hoc LPAC session can collect feedback from experienced LPs who may have dealt with the same issue with other funds in their portfolio.

Emerging VCs should assemble an LPAC and use it. The LPs do not expect you to have all the answers and will probably be happy to help you shape your firm. Three questions that you can pose to the LPs are:

- What do they want to see more of?

- Are they willing to help solve any pressing problems?

- And what can you do to better serve their needs?

Winding Up

How should you follow through on what was promised during fundraising?

Did you make any promises during the fundraising process that your LPs will track? Did you say you would rebrand? Did you say you would add another partner to your team? If you made a promise, you need to follow through. LPs want to invest with individuals who can manage the success of their firm. Do not promise anything you cannot deliver during the course of the fund, especially if you have engaged institutional LPs that will monitor your progress before your next fundraising effort.

Why should you expect to always be fundraising?

Expect LPs to be always conducting diligence on you and your fund. They may seek references about you even when the fund is not being raised. LPs may also use the performance numbers you disclose as a benchmark for other funds or asset classes. They may meet with other LPs, VCs, and entrepreneurs, asking about the quality of their interactions with you and your venture capital firm.

The best LPs constantly monitor their investments and try to understand how you, the VC, are performing over time. Once you raise a fund, you are always raising a fund.

Compendium: Key Takeaways

Over the course of this book, I have tried to introduce you to the central aspects of raising a venture capital fund. Before you begin fundraising, you have to reflect on whether assuming the long-term commitment of raising and managing a venture capital fund is really for you.

Once you have made that critical decision, then you must craft your strategy and tell your story about what value you can add to the venture ecosystem. Then, you start assembling fundraising materials in preparation for fundraising. At this point, you also start assembling a list of LPs.

During the fundraising process, you reach out to LPs, refine your pitch, and hone your fundraising skills. I have described tactics that may be helpful during this part of the journey. I also discussed what to expect during a typical due diligence process, including how LPs will review the operations of your firm. This lets you prepare and, it is hoped, run a tighter ship, allowing you to devote more time to investing and helping your portfolio companies.

I described how to interact with LPs, how to build a limited partner base (LP base), and how to negotiate the Limited Partnership Agreement (LPA). I also gave some pointers on how to simplify the logistics of closing a venture capital fund.

Lastly, I briefly gave some pointers on how to engage with LPs in advance of the next fundraising effort, given that the traditional venture capital model calls for raising funds every couple of years.

Each fundraising process will be different, so I have outlined a general process for how to raise a venture capital fund. This process will, of course, not be the same for everyone, taking different twists and turns. It is hoped that this book will be a compass for your journey.

Learning from history, avoiding mistakes, and building on the experience of others leads to success. If you have feedback, please email me at winter@oper8r.io with anything you find unclear or incorrect, and I'll do my best to incorporate for a second edition.

Nothing in this book should be construed as legal advice. It is simply meant to serve as one way of thinking through raising a first-time fund, which hopefully is made a little less daunting by the prior pages.

Wishing you success in the fundraising and firm-building journey,

Winter Mead

Epilogue

This book is focused on fundraising for a first-time fund only, and some of the information may be relevant for others raising non-first-time funds.

There is a whole world beyond just raising the first fund. Most investors would agree that raising the first fund is just the beginning of a long journey building an investment firm. The journey continues with investing in companies, scaling out the operations of the firm, and building the team and organization.

Given that this book is only meant to serve as an introduction to raising a venture capital fund, there are a lot of things this book is not, including:

- How to be an angel investor
- How to invest like a VC
- How to co-invest with VCs
- How to source, pick, and/or win great investments as a VC
- How to add value and/or exit your portfolio companies as a VC
- How to monitor the portfolio
- VC portfolio risk management
- Innovative models to raise a VC fund

In particular, there are also a number of processes, procedures, and systems that should get implemented when raising a first-time fund that this book doesn't cover comprehensively.

If you're interested in going deeper into the topics mentioned throughout the book, please reach out to me at winter@oper8r.io.

Best,

Winter Mead

Appendix Terms

Accredited investor: defined by securities laws, an accredited investor is an individual or business entity with a certain net worth or income level that is allowed to invest in venture capital funds.

Advisory board: an official advisory committee put in place by the GP and made up of one or more LPs with the purpose of advising the GP with difficult decisions related to fund structure, investments, or other organizational matters.

Anchor limited partner: also known as an anchor LP, the anchor limited partner is the limited partner that first commits to the venture capital fund. Many times, the anchor LP is known by other LPs as being a successful LP investor, and therefore the anchor LP can have influence in convincing other LPs to invest in the venture capital fund.

Annual report: the report a GP discloses annually to its LP case that includes updates with respect to the GP and its portfolio companies.

Blind pool: see Limited Partnership. This is another name for the venture capital fund; it is referring to the fact that the limited partner does not see any of the companies they are investing into when they invest in the Limited Partners hip. Unlike other investments where you know the investment you are investing in, in a venture capital fund, the LP only knows the fund strategy and what the GP is expected to invest in; therefore, the LP is "effectively" blind at the start of the fund's life.

Capital call: capital calls can also be referred to as a draw down. A capital call is a request made by the General Partner (see General Partner) to the limited partner (see limited partner) to pay a certain amount of committed capital (see limited partner Commitment) to the General Partner. Because when a limited partner makes its limited partner Commitment, she does not pay all of the committed capital at once, the General Partner "calls the capital" when the General Partner needs to pay management fees or invest in a new start-up or company.

Capital commitment: see Capital Call.

Carried interest: carried interest is a share of the profits that is paid to the General Partner (see General Partner). Carried interest for venture capital funds can be between 0% and 30% of the profits, though it is typically 20%. For example, a $100 million venture capital fund that makes $100 million in profits (so has generated $200 million in net value) will receive $20 million in carried interest. The equation is carried interest (20%) times net profits ($100 million) equals $20 million. There are typically two ways a General Partner makes money—management fees (see Management Fee) and carried interest.

Carry: see Carried Interest.

Commitment: see limited partner Commitment.

Committed capital: see limited partner Commitment.

Consultant: consultant is a general term referring to a financial advisor that can help the GP raise capital from LPs in the consultant's network. Consultants can sometimes be referred to as Private Placement Agents or Placement Agents.

Data room: a data room is a space (often online) that is shared by the GP to share secure and confidential information with the LP. The data room can also by physical, though this is rarely seen in venture capital.

Due diligence: due diligence refers to the diligence process that occurs between the General Partner (see General Partner) and limited partner before the limited partner (see limited partner) decides to invest in the Limited Partnership (see Limited Partners hip).

Due diligence questionnaire (DDQ): the due diligence questionnaire is a document created by the GP. It has both questions and answers that are helpful for the LP in getting a comprehensive understanding of the venture capital fund, including details about the team, strategy, and operations of the venture capital fund. A DDQ is one of the main documents disclosed by the GP to the LP during the due diligence process, though not all venture capitalists produce DDQs because it is not a legal requirement.

Fiduciary duty: a very important concept that is the legal and ethical duty to act in the best interest of your investor. A GP has the obligation, or fiduciary duty, to act legally and ethically on behalf of the LP

Firm: see Venture Capital Firm.

Fund: see Limited Partnership.

Fundraising: fundraising refers to the period of time when a General Partner (see General Partner) seeks funding for a venture capital fund. This period of time is when the GP will engage consistently with Limited Partners (see limited partner) with the intention of convincing LPs to invest in the venture capital fund.

General partner: General Partners are venture capitalists. General Partner is a term that is interchangeable with GP or venture capitalist. General Partner is the legal term for venture capitalist; thus, some people use the term General Partners to refer to venture capitalists. In this book, I will use these terms interchangeably. So if you see General Partner, GP, VC, or venture capitalist, note that they are all referring to the same thing. General Partners are the ones who find and invest in companies and sometimes sit on the Board of Directors of the companies they invest in. General Partners are also the decision-makers of the venture capital fund, which means the GPs make decisions about the operations, hiring/firing, investing, and investment exit decisions.

GP commitment: the General Partner will invest in the Limited Partnership, and this is known as a General Partner Commitment, or GP commitment. Typically, the GP commitment will equate to 1% to 2% of the total capital committed to the venture capital fund, though sometimes GPs will put in more capital, especially if they are confident in generating strong performance.

Key person clause: the key person clause, formerly known as the key man clause, is a clause in the LPA (see Limited Partnership Agreement) that if triggered, it prevents the GP from making new investments in the venture capital fund.

Legal due diligence (LDD): legal due diligence is part of the due diligence process for raising a venture capital fund. It refers to the negotiation and legal review that happens before a limited partner invests in a venture capital fund. A limited partner can work with a third-party law firm to review the LPA (see Limited Partnership Agreement). A limited partner can also have in-house counsel that can review the LPA to reduce expenses for the limited partner. The goal in legal due diligence is for the LP to protect herself with the terms that will be finalized in the LPA.

Limited partner (LP): Limited Partners are the people and institutions that invest into the General Partners. Examples of Limited Partners include endowments, such as Harvard University or Stanford University, or company, such as Google. They come in all shapes and sizes.

Limited partnership agreement (LPA): the Limited Partnership Agreement is the legal document (or contract) that includes all of the terms of the partnership between the limited partner and General Partner. It is the legal document that is tied to the Limited Partnership, also known as the venture capital fund. Every time a venture capital fund is raised, it will have a new LPA, and some terms may change when the new fund is raised by the General Partner. An LPA is one of the main documents disclosed by the GP to the LP during the due diligence process.

Limited partner base: the limited partner Base is also known as the LP base. This term refers to the collective set of LPs that have invested in a single venture capital fund.

Limited partner commitment: the limited partner commitment, or LP commitment, is the money committed to a venture capital fund. The LP commitment is contractual, and GPs will call this committed capital over time as the GP makes new investments and pays its management fees. Note that this capital is not invested all at once. Rather, it is paid at the time of the capital calls.

Limited partnership (also LP, so don't get confused!): a venture capital fund is also referred to as a VC fund, or just fund. Legally, the structure of a venture capital fund is a Limited Partnership. It is confusing that a VC fund is a Limited Partnership. General Partners, or venture capitalists, manage the day-to-day of the venture capital fund. Limited partners invest in the Limited Partnership. Limited partnerships are "Limited" because all of the investors have limited liability when investing in this type of legal entity.

LP base: see limited partner Base.

Management company: the management company is a legal entity that is set up when raising a venture capital fund. The management company collects the management fees (see Management Fee) from the Limited Partnership and then uses those fees to pay for operational expenses, such as salaries, rent, or business services. The management company is a legal construct created to pay business expenses so that the General Partner is not paying salaries herself.

Management fee: the management fee is the fee paid to the management company by the Limited Partnership (see Limited Partnership) for managing the Limited Partnership. The management fee is typically charged as a percentage of the committed capital to a fund and is typically in the range of 1.5% to 2.5% of commitments, though it can be smaller or larger in exceptional cases. There are typically two ways a General Partner makes money—management fees and carried interest (see Carried Interest). Management fees are paid by the LP regardless of the performance of the venture capital fund.

Most favored nation (MFN): most favored nation is a clause in the LPA (see Limited Partnership Agreement) that gives the LP the right to get the best negotiated term across all of the terms negotiated across all LPs

Non-disclosure agreement (NDA): also known as a confidentiality agreement or confidential disclosure agreement, the NDA is a legal document between the

LP and GP that restricts how the LP can share the GP's information. Typically, LPs will sign some type of NDA before accessing a data room.

Operational due diligence (ODD): operational due diligence is part of the due diligence process for raising a venture capital fund. During operational due diligence, the General Partner discloses information on the operations of the venture capital firm (see Venture Capital Firm) and venture capital fund (see Venture Capital Fund). The limited partner reviews these disclosures and information pertaining to the operations of the firm.

Pitch deck: the slides created by the GP and shared with the LP describing the venture capital fund that the GP is raising.

Pre-marketing: pre-marketing refers to the period of time at the beginning of the fundraising process when the venture capitalist is talking with Limited Partners about the upcoming process of raising the venture capital fund. Pre-marketing is a way for GPs to highlight the investment opportunity and value proposition of the venture capital fund to LPs before beginning the official fundraise process. There is no clear line between the end of pre-marketing and the beginning of the actual fundraising process, though note pre-marketing is used as a tool by the GP to build interest in an upcoming venture capital fundraise.

Private placement agent: also known as just a placement agent. Private placement agents are individuals or firms that help GPs raise capital from LPs by connecting GPs with LPs in the agent's network. Private placement agents take a fee for helping the GP connect with potential LP investors. If successful, private placement agents can decrease the time it takes the GP to raise a venture capital fund.

Private placement memorandum (PPM): the private placement memorandum, usually referred to as the PPM, is a legal document provided to prospective investors that discloses everything a limited partner needs to know to make an informed decision on whether to invest in the venture capital fund. A PPM is one of the main documents disclosed by the GP to the LP during the due diligence process.

Quarterly report: the report a GP discloses quarterly to its LP case that includes updates with respect to the GP and its portfolio companies.

Subscription agreement: a subscription agreement is an application from the LP to join a Limited Partnership. A subscription agreement is filled out by the lawyers of the LPs and are one of the main documents disclosed by the GP to the LP during the due diligence process. Subscription agreements are typically reviewed by the LP during the legal due diligence process when the LP (and her lawyers) is also reviewing the LPA.

VC fund: see Limited Partnership.

Venture capital: venture capital is about financing innovation. Venture capital involves investors investing in start-ups and companies with the expectation that these start-ups and companies will grow to be valuable companies.

Venture capital firm: not to be confused with venture capital fund. Venture capital firm is a general term that refers to the business managed by the venture capitalist. One way to distinguish between venture capital firm and venture capital fund is that a venture capitalist usually only runs one business, but the venture capitalist can raise several venture capital funds over time as part of the venture capital firm.

Venture Capital fund: see Limited Partnership.

Venture capitalist: venture capitalists are also referred to as VCs or General Partners. VC is colloquial and General Partner is the legal term for venture capitalist. Venture capitalists manage the day-to-day of the venture capital fund and are the decision makers with respect to the investments made by the venture capital fund. Additionally, venture capitalists manage the venture capital funds in terms of building the team, making decisions with respect to the operations of the fund, investing in start-ups and companies, and expecting to make a return on their investments in start-ups and companies.

About the Author

Winter Mead has worked in financial services for the better part of a decade at two SEC-registered investment firms and has invested almost $1-billion across 80 private equity and venture capital firms as a Limited Partner, specializing in venture capital. Before becoming an investor, Winter Mead worked in the technology world at three different angel and venture capital financed start-ups. He attended Harvard University and the University of Oxford. Winter was involved with two leading industry organizations: as a member of the National Venture Capital Association (NVCA) and at the committee level of the Institutional Limited Partners Association (ILPA), which sets standards for the private equity industry. In his spare time, he helps teach a course at Stanford University focused on entrepreneurship and venture capital. He is a Chartered Alternative Investment Analyst, which is a professional designation for those specializing in investments such as venture capital.

Lightning Source UK Ltd.
Milton Keynes UK
UKHW010626210921
390952UK00001B/270